CROSSFIRE

*Faith and Doubt in an
Age of Certainty*

CROSSFIRE

Faith and Doubt in an
Age of Certainty

—◆•■•◆—

Richard Holloway

COLLINS
8 Grafton Street, London W1
1988

William Collins Sons & Co. Ltd
London · Glasgow · Sydney · Auckland
Toronto · Johannesburg

BRITISH LIBRARY CATALOGUING IN PUBLICATION DATA

Holloway, Richard, 1933–
Crossfire:
faith and doubt
in an age of certainty
I. Title
284.4

ISBN 0-00-215244-4

First published 1988
© Richard Holloway 1988

Photoset in Linotron Bembo by
Rowland Phototypesetting Ltd
Bury St Edmunds, Suffolk
Made and printed in Great Britain by
William Collins Sons & Co. Ltd, Glasgow

For Sara

CONTENTS

PREFACE

I am sometimes asked by people to help them find faith. Because of what they think I am, they assume that I will be able to persuade them about something they cannot, at present, accept. The converse of this situation is when other people set out to try to prove to me that God does not exist. In each case the assumption is the same. It is assumed that there is, in this area, a secure body of achievable fact which can be mastered, and which those who have mastered it can convey to others. We might call this secure state "certainty", and one of the characteristics of the certain is that they like and are often able to persuade others of their rightness. The paradoxical thing about certainty is that it can be held in absolutely contradictory ways: people are often passionately certain about mutually opposing statements of fact. Now, it would be a simple matter if these contradictions could be theoretically resolved. We know that a thing cannot be round *and* square or black *and* white at the same time, though we also know that people can be deluded about an object's true state. So, we might go on, while we cannot remove people's delusions, we can at least establish facts.

Doubtless that approach works in certain areas, but it clearly does not work in the area of mystery that surrounds the word God. There are no absolutely incontrovertible procedures that seem to be capable of resolving that issue for everyone, for all time. Of course, some people are certain they know what the real facts are, but they are far from being able to establish the certainty of what they are certain about. In fact, when people rehearse their certainties before us they are merely showing us the inside of their own heads, they are not helping us to encounter the mystery for ourselves. Cardinal Newman told us that ten thousand difficulties do not make one doubt, and that is worth remembering; but it is also true that ten thousand certainties do not make one fact.

Ours is an age of certainty, which is why it is such a difficult time for those of us who believe rather than know. We feel uncomfortable in a world that has confidently and certainly established the godlessness of the universe. "How can they really know that?", we ask ourselves; but certainties are harsh and cutting things to throw ourselves upon, so we are left feeling irresolute and out of date. But the same thing can happen in the Church or community of faith itself, because here we can find a similar range of fundamentalisms, similar, at any rate, in the confident certainty with which they are held. And here, again, we may not feel very much at home. Believing for us is being in a kind of mystery and uncertainty. The true medium or habitat of faith is more like water than stone, and believing is more like floating than marching with hobnailed boots on. That analogy is not meant to downgrade faith. After all, floating on ten thousand fathoms of water takes more courage than pounding round the parade ground of modern certainties.

Readers of this book won't find many certainties in it, and it won't teach them how to swim either, but I hope they may get from it some sense of what it is actually like to be in the water. If it is for anyone, it is for those who want to find the courage to live by faith in an age of certainty. It is for those who don't want reverence before mystery crushed out of them, though they are living in an age of stone. Several times in the book I have used John Keats' famous and enigmatic definition of Negative Capability – *when man is capable of being in uncertainties, Mysteries, doubts, without any irritable reaching after fact and reason* – as a sort of answering theme to Faith. I suppose that, in a kind of a way, this book *is* some sort of answer to those who have asked me to help them find faith, though all that any of us can do when asked that is to show our friends that we know there is nothing solid to hold us up, but that we actually do manage to float without being afraid.

I am particularly grateful to Andrew Wilson and Cathy Wilson (who are not related) for much good advice on the first three chapters; and to my secretary, Christine Roy, for all her labours on my behalf, and especially for typing several drafts of this book. I am glad to be able to dedicate the book to my daughter Sara, who will know why.

RICHARD HOLLOWAY
Edinburgh,
October 1987

Part One

THE WHITE GARDEN

Negative Capability, that is when man is capable of being in uncertainties, Mysteries, doubts, without any irritable reaching after fact and reason.

Letter of John Keats to George and Tom Keats
(No. 45)

I

THE WHITE GARDEN

This book is an attempt to give a personal account of the Christian religion, to show the way in which one man holds it. It could begin anywhere, but I want to start it where I am. I am writing it in my study, a small room on the first floor of my house. Outside the window there is a large wild cherry tree, through which the summer rain is dripping. I often gaze into that tree, because I find its greenness consoling. A few minutes ago, my head resting on my left hand as I looked at the tree, I caught sight of a chiffchaff or willow warbler, flitting from branch to branch, a visitor from the wood on the hill a mile away. The sight of the tiny bird, no more than four inches long, hopping among the wet leaves, produced a certain mood in me. As an event it was almost below measurement in significance. It lasted for seconds. I caught brief sight of a tiny, rather shy bird, whose life expectancy was probably only about a year, but that glimpse set off something within me that is close to the experience we call religion.

Religion is a mysterious word, whose origins are obscure, but there is a lot to be said for taking it in a straightforward way. For religious people, however they arrive at the conviction, the world is not all there is and is not only what it seems to be. For all people, religious or not, the world is a bit of a riddle. They look into the distance and muse about life. They are able to reflect on what has happened to them, and they have a particular need to look ahead into the future. And they know that one day they will die. If they read or listen to stories, they will often muse about lives that were once lived and have now disappeared from time, unless they are remembered by friends or have been written about in books. It seems to be death that gets us thinking. If there were no death in front of us, we would probably not ponder about the meaning of life, because there would be nothing to concentrate our minds. There being no end to look forward to, either with fear or resignation, we would live with less self-consciousness. We sometimes imagine that this is how the animals live, if we believe they do not possess reflective self-consciousness. They appear to live unself-consciously in the present moment, simply doing what they do. It might be a bit like that for immortal men and women: there would be no need to muse on the brevity and arbitrariness of life or on the mysterious change wrought in human nature by death. Life might still be a bit of a puzzle for some people who wondered where it came from, but most people would do what they try to do now: live for the moment, getting through the time with as much pleasure or significance or diversion as possible. It is death that spoils things, even for the unreflective. Death limits our lives and makes them precious to us.

Death makes our lives fragile and precious, but it also makes them mysterious. What kind of being is it that can reflect upon its own life, its origin and its end, and then cease to be? Most people face death stoically, but I have seen enough of it to know that few people go to it willingly. At the end, for all but really passionate believers, there is fear to face and shock and surprise: "Wait a minute! I'm not done yet!", is the sort of protest that rises in the throat. But death is not at our command. It comes when we least expect it or want it, catching us in the middle of something. We particularly resent it if it catches us young or if it takes away from us people we love. We know, of course, that death is essential in the world as it is presently constituted, but we look upon it as a thief, out to steal from us what is most precious to us: life.

The brevity of our lives and the silence and blankness of the hereafter cause us to question our existence. We try to understand our own lives. In particular, we want to know why death surprises us. And we are not just thinking of the way death jumps out at us. The real surprise of death is the way it conflicts with something in us that feels immortal, some faint memory from somewhere that persuades us a mistake is being made. It may very well be that there is nothing behind this sensation except ordinary reluctance to leave a good party too soon, but there is enough in the experience to make some people probe a little further. To put it at its lowest: the brevity and the preciousness of life, the surprise of death and the ability we have to reflect upon the meaning of our own existence, all combine, in some people, to produce a mood or disposition that is vaguely religious. It is akin to the sense we sometimes get on entering a house, which ought to be empty, that someone is there. We are aware of a sort of prickling discomfort that points to the presence of someone. A search may prove us wrong or it may prove us right, but the sensation that preceded the search is certainly a fact, and it is analogous to what I have called a "disposition that is vaguely religious". A surprisingly large number of people possess this sense that there is something else there. They become persuaded that the world is not all there is and is not only what it seems to be. And that brings me back to the chiffchaff in the tree outside my window.

Why should the glimpse of that little bird have moved me so much? There were doubtless many elements in the experience, but the thing I am trying to pinpoint at the moment is a sudden stab of awareness that seemed to be more than visual. As a matter of fact, I did not know what kind of bird I was looking at, and had to check it in a book, but my ignorance may have contributed to the mood I am trying to describe, because I was not able immediately to categorize the bird or put it in its place. For a few seconds I was drawn into an awareness of the mysteriousness of things and I had a moment of wonder, focused on the tiny, hopping bird in the tree outside my window.

I had a similar experience of much greater intensity in the famous garden at Sissinghurst in Kent one summer afternoon. Harold Nicolson and Vita Sackville-West bought Sissinghurst Castle in 1930, and over the years that followed until their deaths (Vita's in 1962, Harold's in 1968) they created one of the most perfect and haunting gardens in Europe. Nigel Nicolson has described it in this way:

Harold made the design; Vita did the planting. In the firm perspectives of the vistas, the careful siting of an urn or statue, the division of the garden by hedges and walls and buildings into a series of separate gardens, the calculated alternation between straight lines and curved, one can trace his classical hand. In the overflowing clematis, figs, vines and wistaria, in the rejection of violent colour or anything too tame or orderly, one discovers her romanticism. Wild flowers must be allowed to invade the garden; if plants stray over a path, they must not be cut back, the visitor must duck; rhododendrons must be banished in favour of their tender cousin, the azalea; roses must not electrify, but seduce; and when a season has produced its best, that part of the garden must be allowed to lie fallow for another year, since there is a cycle in nature that must not be disguised. It is eternally renewable, like a play with acts and scenes: there can be a change of cast, but the script remains the same. Permanence and mutation are the secrets of this garden.[1]

I love the countryside and growing-things, but I am not very knowledgeable about them. Most of the common trees of Britain I know, but only a few of the flowers and shrubs. That afternoon I wandered round Sissinghurst in a state of drowsy, yet intoxicated ignorance. I was particularly moved by what is called *The White Garden* and it was there that I had another of these vaguely religious experiences. It was a complex experience, but I was able to separate several of the elements as I tried to analyse it.

The most obvious element was a sense of awe, tinged with surprise, that such intricate and fragile beauty should even exist. I suppose this is what we call a sense of wonder, a sort of joyous incredulity that the loveliness is there at all. It sometimes helps to define an experience by noticing its opposite. In this case the other side of the coin would have been a surly indifference that took the beauty absolutely for granted, which would have been close to the sort of criminal neglect we condemn in parents who are cold and callous towards their children. We would feel that such persons were unnatural, lacking in some fundamental emotion. We believe that parents should love their children, and that people should feel at least some measure of delight in the presence of beauty. People ought to have some sense of wonder, however undeveloped, but that is only another way of saying that we owe a sense of homage to beauty when we find it.

There was an element of wonder in my experience in The White Garden, then, but it was mysteriously tinged with sadness at the same time. It was very like the sudden arousal of romantic desire for a perfect stranger seen at a street corner or turning in at a door. There is something in us that makes us yearn towards others, even if the yearning is often a false idealization of them, the phenomenon we call "falling in love". It is so common that we take it for granted, but it is really as surprising as beauty, when we come to analyse it. Part of the experience is a longing to possess the other, uncover the mystery of her being, somehow attach her to oneself. The difficulty is two-fold. In the first place, we never really can possess the other, even if we are married to her. The intense phase of idealization, of absolute yearning, passes because we discover that the mystery eludes us, leaps away from us. The relationship that has been started can only now continue if the fascination is succeeded by friendship. The second difficulty is that we cannot pursue all the beloved strangers who provoke the yearning in us, mainly because that would damage or destroy the relationships that demand our commitment; but also because we dimly recognize that what we long for is not really in the people who captivate us but only comes through them. My experience in The White Garden had something of the elusiveness of romantic yearning, and that elusiveness consists of a strong desire to be at one with the thing longed for, while recognizing the unrealizability of the longing: how can a man uncover the mystery of a garden's beauty and attach it to himself?

The final element in the experience was a sense of latency or hiddenness in the Garden. It was hard to say whether it suggested presence or absence to me. Maybe Vita Sackville-West and Harold Nicolson had so impressed their personalities on the Garden that it was, in some sense, haunted by them. It felt less specific than that to me, however. The Garden seemed to be waiting for something to quicken it into a different sort of life, and that was strange, because it was already alive with bees and birds and heavy with scent.

The phrase that suggests itself to me to encompass the whole experience is "magnificent incompleteness". There was a wonderful promise in that mysterious complex of reactions that hit me at Sissinghurst, but something, and I do not know what it was, was not delivered. It was the experience of a riddle, the experience of life itself. And this sense was heightened when I climbed the steps of the tower to look at the room where Vita did her writing. It was empty, but it spoke strongly of her presence. On her desk, in a bowl, was an assortment of implements of the sort that writers use; there was an old, leather-bound blotter, closed now, and pictures of Harold Nicolson and Virginia Woolf flanked a row of beautifully bound books; there was a tapestry on the wall, and a famous painting; there were Persian rugs on the floor, and books everywhere, all waiting the return of someone vivid and complex, who died in 1962. The wonder is that that arresting personality has just ceased to be. All the clues to her existence survive still: the Garden and house at Sissinghurst; her books and papers; her writing room, which looks ready for her to walk through the door; but death has taken her away. Death is very much a part of the riddle; death which empties the city.

My experience in The White Garden was really a distillation of my experience of life. All the elements in the riddle were there. First of all, there was an underlying mood of joy and wonder. Joy is a sort of quiet energy that responds eagerly to the very fact of being alive. It is there in all healthy people, but it can be stimulated by particular circumstances, such as a good meal and a bottle of wine, the most basic of stimulants, right up to a varied range of experiences that can include choral evensong heard in a country cathedral late on an Autumn afternoon as dusk gathers; a band marching in a town square followed by a procession of children and dogs; the first glimpse of a beloved child coming home after a long absence. For some it is the first daffodil in Spring that revives their joy; for others it is the living room prepared for Christmas, with coals blazing in the grate. It can be anything that is innocent and straightforward, unaffected by the human tendency to complicate and vitiate. It is true that behind an apparently simple and clear effect like choral evensong or a lovely garden there lies a lot of human complexity, but the effect itself is mysteriously simple and pure, and calls to something in us that recognizes life and responds with a surge of joyous acknowledgement. We probably see it best in children who respond to life immediately, with no premeditation or arranging of attitudes. Joy is our instinctive response to life, and it can surprise us even in the midst of sorrow. In the White Garden I felt a surge of straightforward joy.

But I felt something that was more obscure. I have called it wonder, the kind of sensation that usually leads to those expostulatory words that do not mean anything beyond the mood they express: "Ah!" "Gosh!" "Wow!" Maybe even, "Alleluia!" The first part of the reaction, as these expressions would indicate, is clearly a response to an impact, a shock of some sort, a sudden coming to a halt, because our attention has been grabbed. In fact, it can be very like a quick blow to the midriff, causing us to halt in our tracks and expel air at the same time. But there is a cognitive element in the experience as well. It makes us seek meaning. In fact, we begin to wonder about things. The universe has become something we no longer take for granted or regard with careless eyes. It has become mysterious to us. It seems to contain a secret. There is just a hint of something behind it. At any rate, it begins to puzzle us. "Why is there something and not just nothing? Why does it have this complicated impact on me? It promotes not only joy and wonder; after a while it speaks of sorrow and loss, and I can see now that everything dies, as I shall die."

The most mysterious element in my moment in The White Garden was precisely this sense of loss and the presence of death. Sorrow and a nagging sense of incompleteness are more surprising reactions than joy and wonder, but they were strongly present and have to be reckoned with. And they are strongly present in life. Loss and longing are closely related, and it is often hard to tell which we suffer from. We can feel a sense of loss because it is difficult to hold on to things like youth and beauty and love, or because we have found that we have lived our lives, perhaps unconsciously, on the principle of pursuit: we are after something that is ahead of us, and it stays ahead of us, so that time and life are actually spent in a state of delayed actualization: we spend the voyage up in the prow of the ship looking for land, but it always seems to recede before us. For many people this experience is bitterly empirical. They work hard all their lives, bringing up children, saving their pennies, making plans, looking forward to "enjoying retirement", as they say, when disease or death pounces on them just as they are about to step ashore. That is not the only experience of loss, however. It can come in one of the modes of longing in which we reach towards some object of desire that constantly eludes our grasp. The most puzzling part of this experience comes when you actually attain the object of desire, and continue to feel the sense of loss, because the object of desire turns out to be less than you hoped, or because you have come to realize that what you long for does not seem to exist except in hints and symbols.

The final element in this complex of sensations that made up the experience in The White Garden was a strongly contradictory awareness that something was present and absent at the same time. I knew that Harold Nicolson and Vita Sackville-West were the creators of the Garden in the immediate sense, but to a certain extent they were only arranging into a specific pattern a beauty that was there before them and has survived them. The very ordering of flowers, shrubs and trees into such intricate patterns of loveliness, in which wildness and disorder were a part of the design, promoted a strong sense of latency or presence, though presence is too firm a description. The Garden prompted the question of origin: ultimately, or in the final analysis, how do we account for this extraordinary creation? The question was tantalizing because it suggested both presence and absence to me, but each of these sensations is interesting. A sense of the presence of something obviously fits if there is a reality behind the universe that is somehow connected to it, what I have called the feeling that the world is not all there is and is not only what it seems to be. The discovery and understanding of that presence is the impulse behind religion, but its apparent opposite is just as interesting and may even point in the same direction. After all, we can only experience the absence of something if we have, in some way or other, known its presence. This is the most tantalizing aspect of religion: it goes on haunting us even when we think we have discarded it. That sense of absence may even be more potent than the sense of presence, because it promotes longing and heart-hunger and a kind of sorrow; and how are we to account for these things in a universe that is empty of transcendence and is

24

only what we can see, feel and measure? However we decide
the question, it is the question we are born asking and may
spend our lives seeking to answer: *Is there anybody out there?*

The White Garden concentrated for me in a particularly
vivid way all the responses that life prompts. I experienced
joy, and wonder at the beauty that prompted the joy. I
experienced sorrow and a mysterious sense of loss, because
the beauty that was before me somehow eluded the very
longing it had created in me. Finally, I was not sure whether
I was in the presence of another reality that was living and
could relate to me or whether I was simply mourning its
absence. That complex of emotions could be described as the
essential prelude to religion, if there is something beyond this
world that seeks to communicate with us through this world.
If there is nothing beyond us, nobody here but ourselves,
then this complex of emotions defines the essential tragedy
of humanity, because we are filled with longings that cannot
be fulfilled, and are prompted to ask questions whose answers
only increase our sorrow. The particular solution we choose,
or are chosen by, is what we loosely call a Faith. Faith is
not believing ten impossible things before breakfast every
morning. Faith is the decision to choose one or other of the
answers that we find in human history to the question of life's
meaning. It is called Faith because, in the nature of the case,
there can be no leading of absolute proof on one side or the
other: we cannot absolutely determine the rational certainty
of the presence of something beyond ourselves, and it is even
more difficult to demonstrate the certainty of an absence of
anything. We are left, therefore, with a calculated probability
on the basis of which we act, and that action is called Faith.
As we say, we *believe* in God or we believe that God does not
exist.

And we ought to note one other characteristic of Faith: it is
a condition that is inevitably accompanied by doubt, precisely
because rational certainty is not available to it. Doubt is
always a descant on Faith, as Geddes McGregor put it once,
and it works on any kind of Faith. Believers often doubt the
Faith that God exists, and unbelievers often doubt the Faith
that God does not exist.

Life is a riddle, and there seem to be various ways of

responding to it. If the riddle poses the question: *Does life mean anything?* we can decide that it does have meaning, on the basis of information or intelligence we derive from the universe itself; clues or hints that, if we read them correctly, point us in the direction of a transcendent solution. The explication of that answer and the human response to it is broadly what we mean by religion, and one particular version of that response will be the broad topic of this book. Or we can decide that there is no evidence that life has any ultimate meaning: it simply is. Admittedly, it is rather mysterious that there is something and not just nothing, but the puzzling aspects of life do not in themselves admit of any transcendent answer. The universe is absurd in the final analysis, giving rise to creatures with a need for meaning and a fear of death and absolute extinction in a world ultimately without meaning in which everything is on the way to death. But it is possible to give such a world personal significance by the way we live in it. The voyage we are on may be our last, but that is no reason for not enjoying it while it is happening. And even if we cannot find any absolutely incontrovertible evidence for feeling that we ought to increase good things rather than bad things while we are on the voyage, there is a sort of commonsense obviousness about it which makes it compelling. I do not need a solemn command from the universe to tell me that it is better not to hurt people, for instance. And it also seems only fair to try to help those whose place on the ship is much less comfortable than mine. After all, there is much to be said for loving one another before we die. Inevitably, on such a voyage there will be some wistfulness and melancholy to contend with, especially towards the end as the days shorten and we get within sight of port, but cheerfulness will keep breaking in and, like everyone else, we'll learn to endure the prospect of our going hence.

I have a great deal of respect for the attitude of wistful stoicism outlined in the last paragraph, and it sometimes corresponds to my own mood. Nevertheless, it is not the particular type of faith to which I have committed my life; but, before going on to attempt some sort of account of that faith, there is another topic I'd like to explore briefly as I conclude this chapter, and that is the mysterious way in which a faith is chosen. Robust believers often challenge other people to have faith, and that challenge is one of the puzzles we must explore later on, but a challenge to believe is, on the face of it, an odd thing to make. We either believe or we do not. Faith is possible for us or it is not, though in putting it this way I am already altering what I have said about faith: which is that any of the choices we make in attempting to answer the question of life's meaning is, in some sense, a faith, because there is no possibility of achieving irrefutable proof in support of any of the possible responses we might make. Nevertheless, people tend to limit the word "faith" to the position adopted by those who opt for the religious answer, which I have defined loosely as *believing that the world is not all there is and is not only what it seems to be.* There is a lot to be said for limiting the word in this way, especially when we come to explore the layers of meaning in the word itself, so we might conveniently settle the matter of language by using the rather neutral word *belief* to describe the three attitudes I have outlined as responses to the question of life's meaning: the religious belief that there is something beyond the universe that gives meaning to it; the strong belief that there is nothing beyond us and the physical universe; and the vague uncertainty about the whole issue that probably characterizes most people in the West today, resulting in a sort of good-natured hedonism that tries to make the most of life, while avoiding injury to other people. If we describe each of these three attitudes as a belief, the voluntary acceptance of a particular account of the meaning of the universe, we can limit the word *faith* to the first type of belief, because it implies, or ought to imply, a much more radical decision than the others, and one that influences every department of life. Unlike the other two beliefs, religious belief or faith will lead to specific actions that will often go against common sense or conventional wisdom. A parable might help to explain this.

Let us suppose there are three men marooned on a small island that seems to be far from anywhere. On the island there is enough fruit to ensure survival and enough cover to ensure shelter. It will be possible to live there quite comfortably and even create enough diversions to help pass the time.

Mist surrounds the island and the men sometimes think they hear a voice that tells them they can find a way out if they will go to a particular point and plunge into the water, where a powerful current will bring them, admittedly after a hazardous swim, to the mainland. Each of the men adopts a different attitude. One man believes that the voice is a delusion and that there is no escape from the island, whose limitations they must stoically endure. One man is not quite sure what to believe, but he quite enjoys life on the island and finds enough to keep himself distracted. The other man cannot quite believe that the voice is unreal and he is not able to ignore the issue and settle down on the island, so he decides to trust the voice. That act of belief will involve him in a radical act of faith: he will have to throw himself into the sea, through the mist, trusting that he will find the current and be carried to the mainland. His belief, in other words, will call for radical action and trust of a high order. Faith, unlike the other two forms of belief, will involve the believer in high risk. In order to test the truth of the voice that calls him he will have to embark on a hazardous course of action that will separate him from his two companions and their accustomed routines.

That is a partial analogy of faith. Unlike the other two beliefs, faith does not accept things the way they are or the way they appear to be. The man or woman who chooses faith chooses, in theory, to be different, to march to the sound of an unseen but insistent drummer, and that march may lead the person of faith into situations of discomfort and deprivation. It may even lead to death. Faith presumes the existence of an invisible and intangible reality whose demands often run counter to the ordinary pleasures and loyalties of life. But why is the making of this choice a matter for so much disagreement, argument and dispute? It would seem to be a matter of plain sense that you cannot force yourself to believe anything, no matter how much you'd like to. How, then, are the choices made?

The choice that probably needs the least explanation is the easy-going non-belief that characterizes the average person in the Western liberal democracies today. This sort of non-belief is invasive and subtly powerful. It seems to characterize reasonably affluent and moderately contented people in highly technological societies. Such people have most things under control, and life is pleasant for them, on the whole. They do not probe too deeply beneath the surface, and they see little point in asking what seem to be unanswerable questions. A sociologist has called this prevailing mood *disenchantment* and the word captures the situation exactly. The universe has been purged of wonder. The White Garden is only one of an infinite series of sensations now available. It is part of the tour, but we can only allot it thirty minutes, so "hurry along, please, the driver is waiting". Wonder can only be engendered in a life that is not filled to the edges. Wonder is a slow and shy thing that needs lots of silence and space in which to grow. We purged the poor of wonder in the nineteenth century by enslaving them to the Industrial Revolution and unceasing labour. Some aspects of the Technological Revolution of the second half of the twentieth century seem to have purged wonder from us all, with their constant sound and surveillance and sensation. So the prevailing belief-system in places like Britain or America, for instance, is what I have called "good-natured hedonism", from the Greek word for pleasure. The pursuit of pleasure has always been a strong element in developed societies, though it originally characterized only the wealthy or ruling classes. Today it has been democratized, but its identifying marks remain the same. Its main usefulness lies in its power to distract, and distraction is a necessity for the bored. Boredom seems to characterize those who are uncommitted or uninvolved. It is the mark of those who would be described by air traffic controllers as being "in a holding pattern". If we may pursue the metaphor, "inflight entertainment" is the perfect modern symbol of the need for and power of distraction. On a long flight passengers have to be distracted with frequent meals, films and music programmes, because they are "on hold" for the duration of the flight. Distraction is the prevailing mood of a culture on hold. It is the way we pass the time between birth and death when life has been purged of its drama and commitment. The pity lies in the fact that the pleasures do not seem able to do their job for long and we end up, in T. S. Eliot's phrase, trying to be "*distracted from distraction by distraction*".

It is, I think, a mistake to moralize about contemporary hedonism and scold its practitioners. The only real cure for boredom is purpose. The dilemma that life thrusts upon us is precisely the question of whether there is any purpose. To condemn people who have no purpose for behaving purposelessly is cruel as well as illogical. If we believe that life is without any final meaning or purpose then we will inevitably find some way of passing the trip with as little pain and as much pleasure as possible. Frank Sinatra once said that he believed in anything that would help him through the night, and it is as good a philosophy as any for a disenchanted universe. It is not surprising that most people, probably without really thinking about it, pursue consolation and distraction in a society that is without purpose, either socially or individually. They find themselves stuck on a mist-encircled island, like a jet plane in mid-flight, and the obvious thing to do is to get into something comfortable, break out the drinks and watch the movie, "distracted from distraction by distraction".

Passionate believers in the absence of God, on the other hand, are a rare and often noble breed. Their commitment to an ultimately meaningless universe can be heroic, especially when they are men and women of compassion. They tell us "naught for our comfort", but their clear-eyed decision to face what they believe to be reality is wholly admirable. The great advantage of their belief, and the thing that makes it most compelling to some, is that they do not have to struggle to explain away the hideousness of human history and sub-human creation. Human history has always been characterized by suffering. Much of it is inflicted by the strong upon the weak, though much of it is mysteriously self-inflicted. The wars, pogroms and massacres of this century, examples of what the American historian Barbara Tuchman calls the human "march of folly", raise tremendous questions against any religious interpretation of human history. These questions are partly answered by the theory that God is in some sense self-limited in order to allow humans real freedom, but that answer does not touch the problem of suffering in the sub-human creation. Rather surprisingly, Evelyn Underhill put it as well as anyone can:

We can't, I think, attribute all the evil and pain of creation to man's rebellious will. Its far-reaching results, the suffering of innocent nature, the imperfection and corruption that penetrate all life, seem to forbid that. The horrors of inherited insanity, mental agonies, the whole economy of disease, especially animal disease, seem to point beyond man to some fundamental disharmony between creation and God. I sympathize a good deal with the listener who replied to every argument on the love of God by the simple question, "What about cancer in fish?"[2]

All these questions are resolved for the atheist. Once we admit the originating absurdity of the universe everything else falls into place and nothing surprises us. Atheism of this sort is a kind of poetry, and it has a noble contemptuousness about it. If the hedonistic non-believer is best thought of as someone pleasantly passing the time on an inter-continental flight, the heroic atheist is like a voluntary victim among the Jews on one of the death-trains to Auschwitz or Buchenwald. He knows where the train will end up, but he refuses to grovel before its guards or dissemble about its destination. Genuine atheists of this sort are few and far between, and I have come to believe that they are mysteriously close to God's heart.

Religious Faith is not an easy thing to maintain in our kind of society, therefore. It is true that many people continue to hold a sort of residual half-belief in a reality beyond the material world, but it is a puzzled and episodic thing, surprising its practitioners with mysterious urges on Christmas Eve, or just after the birth of a child or the death of a friend. Religious Faith may be declining in our society and it may be a difficult thing to hold on to, but it has been a part of human consciousness, as far as we can tell, from the very beginning. It is unwise to reject lightly something as old and as persistent as Religious Faith. As much for my own sake as for anyone else's, therefore, I would like to give a personal account of a Faith that has won the allegiance of some of the most interesting people in history and has shown an amazing facility for renewing itself. It is used to defeat. It was once described as an anvil that has worn out many hammers. It deserves another look.

II

THE ACCUSATION

Late one evening I came out of a concert in the Usher Hall, Edinburgh. Normally on such occasions I wear a collar and tie, but for this particular event I had been invited in my official capacity as Bishop of Edinburgh, so I wore a purple stock and clerical collar. It was a busy night in the city, the streets filled with visitors to the Festival. As I walked along under the shadow of the castle I was still tingling with excitement at the freshness of the performance of Weber's "Oberon" I had just enjoyed. Three animated young men were walking in my direction, slightly the worse for drink but in no sense out of control. For some reason one of them was electrified by my approach. He stopped in his tracks, broke off what he was saying to his friends and came over to me. He took my hand solemnly, looked into my eyes and said, "I want you to know that I think all religion is a sham". His friends called him back and he strode away.

Ministers of religion are often encountered in this way when they are caught sight of in public places, though people are rarely rude when they make us a present of their opinions. In fact, they are more likely to burden us with confidences than with hostility. Nevertheless, a good number of these encounters are likely to be unpleasant, and it becomes quite obvious that religious professionals produce conflicting emotions in people. One of the common perceptions people have of the clergy is that there is something phoney about them, their business is not quite legitimate, and they irresistibly remind confident unbelievers of those snake-oil salesmen who roamed the old West purveying useless mixtures as universal cures. It is obvious that if there is nothing out there, no world beyond this world, then we are consciously or unconsciously fraudulent in our exhortations. Before going any further, therefore, we ought to come to grips with this criticism. If it is true it really cancels the possibility of an honest religion. Is religion a sham?

A sham is a fraud, an act of major pretence, but there can be several shades of meaning in the term. Conscious shams or fraudsters are straightforward quacks or impostors, pretending to a knowledge they know they do not possess. But some fraudsters are victims of delusion, their delusion being the way they neurotically handle some difficult situation. I knew a man who persuaded himself that a woman was in love with him, and he began to pester her. Nothing would persuade him that she did not reciprocate his feelings. If a third party was brought in and the girl swore in front of her that she was not interested in him, he simply fitted that into his delusional scheme: She was saying that to keep the public out of it, because she was not free to be seen with him, but she was truly in love with him. A delusion of that sort is impervious to all evidence, since it cleverly incorporates into its system of reality anything that is said against it.

Yet another sense of the term is found in the popular interpretation of Marx's critique of religion, which sees it as a conspiracy to keep the poor resigned to their lot. Religion is a drug, "the opium of the people", deliberately handed out by those in power so that they can maintain control. Close to this is the Freudian conviction that religion is a projection of our longing for God and immortality onto the blank screen of the universe, which bounces back a God made in our own image to comfort us in our cosmic loneliness. We shall examine this charge in greater detail in a later chapter.

The final sense in which the word is used is probably the most common: religion is a sham because its professors do not live up to it. This version is heard most often in the cry, "the Church is full of hypocrites". Let us look at some of these accusations of fraud and see what truth we can find in them.

Religion as a *conscious* fraud, put over by clever and cynical manipulators of the gullible, is quite rare in cultures where religion is unpopular or persecuted, though it may be more common in places like the U.S.A. where a more general religiosity is common. It is true that American fiction is no stranger to the religious conman, such as Elmer Gantry, who plays cleverly upon human susceptibilities. However, it is hard to tell how often fraud of this sort, in its pure form, exists. I suspect that most religious fraudsters of this sort are, in part at least, self-deceived, or were once sincere but have become corrupt. The existence of this kind of fraudulence, however, does not really tell us anything about the truth of religion, any more than a quack doctor tells us the truth about orthodox medicine. The phenomenon simply reminds us of the varieties of human dishonesty, and there is nothing surprising in that. We have to admit that religion is open to fraudulence of this sort, but that does not amount to definite proof that it is intrinsically fraudulent. To prove that you would have to demonstrate that most religious professionals are in it for money or power and nothing else, and that will be hard to prove. There are clearly men and women of faith in every generation who are led by their faith into danger, suffering, discomfort, loss and death. They may be self-deceived, they may be ultimately mistaken in their commitment, but their self-sacrifice cannot be dismissed as some elaborate sham. If they deceive anyone, it is themselves. Some religious leaders are frauds, but that truism does not tell us anything about the nature of what we might call pure religion, and to understand as well as to oppose anything we ought to address it in its purest form.

The accusation that religion is a *delusion* is very hard to deal with one way or another. In the nature of the case, the claims of the Christian religion can only really be proved or disproved after death. The Christian religion and its accumulated wisdom and insight can be used in a variety of ways to assist daily living, but at the heart of the thing there is a claim that this life is a prelude or preparation for the life to come. Obviously, if it turns out that there is no life to come then the foundational premise of the Christian religion, and most of the other versions of monotheism, will be shown to have been false or delusional. By the same logic, of course, if it turns out that there is a life to come then the foundational premise of materialistic atheism will be shown to be false. The problem for both theism and atheism is that objective proof for either will be reached only after we die. If we cease to exist at death we won't be around to relish the satisfaction of knowing we

were right after all, if we are unbelievers; but if we find that
we are still around after death, it is highly unlikely that
believers will want to spend much time gloating over con-
founded atheists, though I suspect that most of them will
have seen the joke for themselves by that time. However it
turns out, atheists are likely to come off worse: if they are
right, no one is going to be there to give them credit for their
perspicacity, but if they are wrong they are going to be the
first to know it.

Objective certainty on the subject is not available to us in
this life. There is, of course, subjective conviction, but we
have to note that subjective conviction is a private thing,
which, of itself, proves nothing. Since we cannot, in the
nature of the case, know for certain on this side of death what
lies on the other side, there is really no way of absolutely
demonstrating either the delusional nature of religion or its
reality. Religion may be a delusion or a projection of our own
hopes onto the great abyss that awaits us, but it may be a
genuine response to transcendent reality, acting upon us in
the way that the moon influences the sea, creating in our
hearts the ebb and flow of spiritual longing.

The religious question is abidingly fascinating precisely
because the choice of answers is so extreme. Some people
will remember the human capacity for delusion and wishful
thinking, and will operate a stringent method of judgement,
which will lead them to reject the religious answer. They
might argue thus: delusion and unreality are dangerous companions for men and women. If indulged in at all they can
seep into every area. Once we start basing our lives on wishful
thinking and the normal human longing to be significant, we
can slip into other areas of unreality, and we can end up
convinced, if not of our own divinity, at least of our own
almost divine superiority. It is better to have a method of
judgement about such things which is almost invincibly sceptical, since we know how credulous human beings can be.
By operating a principle of radical scepticism we will preserve
ourselves from self-delusion, and if we are proved wrong
after death, it will be a pleasant surprise.

That is one way of resolving the issue, and it will appeal
to people who believe in taking a hard-headed attitude to life:

the burden of proof will always lie with those who are making the unusual claim, and since no real proof will be available it will be better to assume that it does not exist and act accordingly. That is an inviting resolution of the problem posed by religion, but it does not completely dispose of the issue. Most thinking people would probably rather know the truth about the universe, however uncomforting it might be, than follow a fantasy, but the sceptical solution does not necessarily resolve the question of truth. We have already seen that in our society there has been a steady erosion of faith in a transcendent reality, the phenomenon described as "disenchantment", but the prevalence of an attitude does not amount to additional support for its accuracy: it might only serve to bear testimony to the power of fashion, in thought as in everything else. Scepticism is a useful and healthy attitude in many situations, but it can suffer the same corruption as anything human and lead to that strange phenomenon called pyrrhonism, which is the doctrine of the impossibility of attaining certainty of knowledge about anything. Absolute scepticism is incapable of making decisions, and endlessly postpones them. T. S. Eliot pointed out that absolute scepticism can kill a civilization, because *"we need not only the strength to defer a decision, but the strength to make one"*.[1] Credulity is clearly a danger to human beings, because it can dispose them towards an acceptance of the false and bogus. Scepticism can act as a filter which lets truth in, while trying to keep error out, but filters have to be permeable if they are to be of any use. Absolute scepticism is absolutely impermeable to the possibility of transcendence, and that creates a major problem for human beings. It is important for human beings to relate to the real universe and to whatever in that universe is essential to their true development. It is important, for instance, for them to know what substances are noxious and what substances are edible. Absolute scepticism in this area would lead to anorexia, just as absolute credulity would lead to the opposite danger of indiscriminately eating everything in sight. Either attitude is deadly to health. If there is a transcendent or supernatural dimension to the universe, then we need to discover a kind of permeable scepticism that will keep dangerous fantasies out but will let important realities in. We seem to have created a society in the West today that is spiritually anorexic and has become incapable of absorbing or responding to signals of transcendence. It is possible, therefore, that we have created a culture which is spiritually recessive and will become increasingly incapable of responding to part of the reality of the universe.

It is because ours is a spiritually disenchanted society that religion seems to be such a large problem, but in many cultures, where wonder has not been purged from human consciousness, the religious solution to the question of the meaning of life is almost instinctive and universal. The persistence and fact of faith is something that a permeable scepticism will take into account in its examination of reality. It is true that the existence of a longing or appetite does not prove the existence of its satisfaction, but it would be a strange universe that produced longings as wildly unrealistic as the longings of religion unless something out there corresponded to them in some way. What if there is something else there in the universe, a supra-material reality that corresponds to that part of our own nature that transcends our own physical existence? How might such a reality make itself known to us, and how might we respond? These questions will engage us later, but they are perfectly legitimate questions and ones that a wise scepticism will not entirely filter out.

The religious answer to these questions will not satisfy everyone, but there is no reason to suppose that it can never be held with integrity and sincerity. If people are more intent on filtering out error than in receiving truth, however unexpected, then they are less likely to accept the religious account of the facts that confront us as we wrestle with the meaning of things. But others may have a bias that lies more in the direction of receiving the truth than in filtering out error, and they are more likely to be attracted to the account given by religion of the facts that confront us. At this point I am not interested in making a judgement between these two possible attitudes, except to point out that either is justifiable, and neither is intrinsically delusional. Many religious people choose their answer because they think it fits their experience of the facts of life better than any other. All I want to conclude from this fact is that religion may ultimately be wrong, though its practitioners may believe in it for perfectly honest and justifiable reasons. They may be wrong, but they are not necessarily fraudulent in cleaving to it. Religion may be a mistake, therefore, but it is not a sham.

The popular version of the Marxist theory of religion is too elaborate and contrived to be completely convincing, and the facts of history do not really support it. We can concede immediately that religion can be wrongly used to reinforce power, just as marriage can be used to support dynastic arrangements, but we have already seen that the corruption of a thing is no absolute argument against the thing in theory. All human agencies and institutions tend to abuse, but that is because of the weakness and fallibility of human nature, not necessarily because some institutions are intrinsically evil. It is a fact that religion has been used to maintain oppressive structures and social divisions, but this is mainly because major institutions tend to reflect and support the dominant ideas current in the societies in which they are set. In a conservative society religious institutions will reflect conservative values, and in a revolutionary society they will increasingly adjust to the norms of the revolution. But religious institutions are not only reactive to the social and political context in which they find themselves. They have often been found in history challenging the status quo and working for its overthrow, as in South America and South Africa today.

Judaeo–Christian religion has a strong prophetic element within its history, which has prompted some of its most interesting exponents to challenge the powerful institutions of society, often at great cost to themselves. It can be argued that the prophetic tradition in religion is always in the minority, but that is also true of the mystical tradition or the intellectual element. Religion is a complex phenomenon and it is easy, but invariably wrong, to dismiss it on the basis of a selective estimate of its record. The fact remains that it does not operate in only one way in society, and to develop a simple conspiracy theory to account for it will usually be wrong. There *are* conspiracies, and people will use even holy things for their own ends, but human history, including religious history, is more about muddle, accident and failed ideals than about carefully crafted plots. Religion can be, has been and always will be abused, but it can exalt, purify and challenge people, and this is as characteristic of it as the other. There is an invariable tendency in human affairs for ideals and visions to institutionalize themselves. In time the institutions take on a power of their own that is often in conflict with the original vision, though it may not be in total, all-out opposition. Sociologists call this phenomenon "the routinization of charisma", and it is as much a fact in Marxist structures as in Christian institutions. The great tension in all spiritual movements arises because of the conflict between those who have to tend the institution and those who are still captivated by the pure ideal. The embodying of ideals in human structures is invariably complex and can be tragic, but it seems to be unavoidable, given the nature of men and women and their strong impulse to create systems and develop institutions. Part of the drama of human history lies in the permanent struggle to recover purity in the face of this invariable tendency towards complexity and corruption. Religious institutions are subject to this law, but they are no more bound by it than are any other institutions.

Interestingly enough, one of the most trenchant defences of the fundamental honesty of religion is found in George Orwell's interpretation of Marx's famous description of religion as the opiate of the people. In a fascinating new study of Orwell's thought, Patrick Reilly points out that history has turned Marx's original words upside down, thereby converting what was a sympathetic description of religion into a sneer. Reilly tells us:

> The strength of Moscow's appeal is its inheritance, via Marx from the old religion, of the vision of a reconsecrated world where men will live as brothers, as the children of God, even if God is now called dialectical materialism. This is what Marx meant, on Orwell's reading of the famous opium passage. The chief dynamiter of religious civilization did not press the button in careless indifference to the act's gravity; Orwell reprimands those shallow disciples of the master, who, missing the act's temerity, wrench blithely from its context the opium quotation for use in the service

of a reckless atheism. Marx did *not* mean that religion is a dope dispensed from above, like the *soma* of *Brave New World*, to keep its addicts functioning placidly within an unjust order; it is not opium *for* but *of* the people, a drug certainly, but created by the people themselves to supply a need and to mitigate a pain that Marx recognized as very real indeed.

George Eliot may command us to dispense with opiates; the more compassionate Marx neither expects nor admits the need for such fortitude from ordinary human beings. Suffering people will inevitably seek cure or consolation, and here, in this root fact of human nature rather than in the trickery of some exploiting class, is the true origin of religion. Far from being a shameful swindle, religion is the instinctive untutored response to misery, and Marx logically rejects the call to discard all opiates; if the misery of existence causes man's addiction, it is both heartless and pointless to take away the painkiller while leaving the pain. Marx, in effect, salutes religion as the only stay against despair available to man before the arrival of the true redeemer; meanwhile, why expel the priest from the sickroom before the physician arrives? Though denying the truth of religion, Marx concedes its consolatory power and provisional value.

Orwell directs us to the sentence preceding the opium assertion so that we will not get Marx wrong: "Religion is the sigh of the soul in a soulless world." This, properly understood, indicts the brutal world rather than the deluded soul, for man's superiority *is* in possessing a soul which seeks justice, even if the search has hitherto been in the wrong place. Religion is simply socialism gone astray as prescientific man gropes for the truth. Nevertheless, this blind groping is infinitely preferable to a soulless indifference matching a soulless world; religion is a necessary mistake on the road to socialism.[2]

We cannot take too much comfort from Orwell's honest defence of the historic role of religion but it does, I think, absolve religion from the charge that it is intrinsically fraudulent. We can be mistaken and sincere at the same time.

But are we mistaken? Is there nothing out there that corresponds to our longing? There can be no general answer to that question. Each of us must answer the question personally, because it is a question of ultimate, personal concern. But there is also a sense in which it is a question for the whole of humanity. Many individuals in the past have been carried along by a corporate faith, the worldwide view of the society in which they lived. It is one of the paradoxes of our time, however, that we all belong to what an American sociologist has called "the lonely crowd". We all participate in a mass culture that smoothes out differences and imposes a common working philosophy, yet we have never been more atomized as individuals, more separated from each other. The philosophy we absorb gets us all thinking in the same way, but tells us we are on our own. Like passengers on a jumbo jet, we are united in our isolation, joined together in our loneliness. We are all on the same trip, all client-victims of modern technology, but our brief association is accidental and artificial. When we get to Baggage Claim and Customs we all grab our luggage and go our separate ways. One of the pains of modernity is precisely this strange unity in separation. What we have in common is the certainty that there is no longer any common view of meaning or morals that can unite us. If modern jet travel is an apt image of the pampered transience of human life in our part of the globe, then the modern supermarket is a perfect image of the cognitive confusion of human beings today. The only thing that unites us is our right to choose whatever brand we want, but the very excess of choice paralyses us. We are in the state described in the Book of Judges: *In those days there was no king in Israel; every man did what was right in his own eyes.*[3] There is no unifying factor in our experience, no common myth. Out of other periods of cultural disintegration unifying creeds have emerged and it is not inconceivable that it could happen again, but it is certainly not characteristic of our day. We all do what is right in our own eyes; we believe in this or that for a while and move on. We are unquiet spirits, impulse buyers in the great philosophical supermarket.

I have neither the learning nor the inclination to tackle the construction of a new synthesis, but I do want to try to articulate why I believe and what I believe. This book is testimony, witness, rather than argument, though it will inevitably involve itself in argument as it states its case. The tone I would like to achieve is found in a little encounter in John's Gospel, in chapter nine. The Pharisees are questioning the man born blind whom Jesus has healed, and they say to him: "Jesus is a sinner". To which the man replies: "Whether he is a sinner, I do not know; one thing I know, that though I was blind, now I see" (John 9:24b–25). We might call the blind man's attitude confessional minimalism, because it sticks to personally experienced fact and does not hazard an opinion on matters beyond its reach. That is the tone I would like to achieve as I turn to the passenger next to me in midflight and continue my account.

III

THE WINDOW

When I lived in Oxford I used to spend my day off rambling with my dog in the surrounding countryside. Sometimes a friend would join me on a walk and we'd spend the hours talking as we tramped over Otmoor or through the Chilterns. The talk would continue over lunch in a pub, with Sam the dog fixing us with an appealing stare as we munched hunks of cheese and long cuts of French bread, grateful for any scraps that fell from our table, though one friend always insisted on buying him a whole pork pie to himself.

But on many occasions Sam and I were on our own, and on these solitary rambles one place became particularly important to me. I used to cross Port Meadow and walk from Binsey, past the ruins of the nunnery at Godstow and up the road to the village of Wytham. One of my favourite pubs was there, but it was the church at Wytham that really drew me. Sam and I would enter the lovely old church, just outside Wytham Abbey. He would sniff around the place, picking up his own information, while I sat and waited. All Saints, Wytham, is a small church, and I would gather its stillness around me and look at the little window above the altar. It contained an exquisite piece of eighteenth-century stained glass, filled with warm colours, depicting the Adoration of the Shepherds of the Infant Jesus. Stained glass always looks dull and uninteresting from outside a church, but when you enter you see that the light pouring through it from outside brings it to life. I used to think that that was a small parable of the life of faith. From outside, the life of the Church can appear to be very dull and uninteresting, but when you enter and sit and wait, all sorts of things come to life, and through light you see light. But the experience of sitting in Wytham Church was more than the source of that rather obvious preacher's device. The Adoration of the Shepherds came to life because light poured through it. Something came to it from outside that gave it meaning.

So far I have been tentative and discursive in what I have written, and some readers may have been irritated as they watched me circling the subject, apparently reluctant to pounce on it. In fact, I am trying to establish a mood, create a disposition in the reader. Confident things are frequently written for and against religion, but this very confidence may be the greatest hazard we face in coming to terms with the thing itself. We are dealing with mystery, and the appropriate response to mystery should be humbler than religion's detractors or protectors often show themselves to be. When we start meditating on life, either because we are stung into it by some sorrow or joy, or because it has become the habit of a lifetime, we confront something elusive and puzzling. Life does not seem to bear its own explicit meaning within itself; nor does the universe offer us an account of its causes, if there are any, or of its purpose, if there is one. We are left to interpret the riddle by ourselves, and riddle it is. We find ourselves in the midst of history, uncertain whether the universe is self-generating, and therefore an end in and to itself, or created and therefore related to an end beyond itself. But the puzzle is about more than the origin of the universe; we ourselves are often a riddle to ourselves. If my experience in the White Garden was in any way representative, we are haunted by longings we cannot entirely explain, and troubled by experiences that convey both a sense of presence and a sense of absence. Like an amnesiac we are tantalized by dreams we do not know how to interpret. Are they delusions, false comforters in the face of loss, or are they genuine signals from the mystery that besets us?

How can we decide this question, without being offered irrefutable proof? Unless we can plunge our hands into the divine wounds we will not believe. And who can blame us for this caution? So there grows up a vast intellectual enterprise to provide us with reasons for taking the leap of faith or for staying where we are. We end up like Robert Browning's Grammarian, who decided that *"before living, he'd learn how to live . . . he'd image the whole, then execute the parts"*.[1] But that is precisely what we are never allowed to do. We never can find verbal equivalents for the mysterious reality that obsesses us. We want to fix the rules for the enterprise or even establish that there are rules, but nothing we do seems to give us the advantage we want. As long as we stay on the outside trying to figure out the design on the window, willing the mystery to turn itself inside out so that we can decide whether it is worth entering, we shall remain baffled. But even when we move over the threshold and decide to enter we must learn to accept an enduring degree of elusiveness in the mystery we are pursuing. It will not be controlled or interrogated; it cannot be taken by force. Waiting is what we have to learn to do, because revelation is the mode of approach the mystery adopts towards us, and revelations have to be waited for, they can never be controlled.

The inclusive term for the basic material religion invites us to study is "revelation". I have already alluded to one of the senses of the term in my description of the light that poured through the window in Wytham Church. In revelation something is made visible that was previously obscure, light is thrown on it. Another sense of the word is to unveil or uncover something that is hidden. In the Old Testament it is sometimes used with a sexual reference, as in Ezekiel, where Israel is castigated for exposing her naked body in fornication.

In revelation two things seem to be happening. There is, first of all, an event that is to some extent objective, external to or over against the self. The "event" may be a historical episode interpreted by meditation, it may be a story, a parable or poem, it may be a person or even a place. Whatever it is, it becomes a means of revelation to us; through it we catch sight of the mystery that is hidden from us and light is cast upon our own condition. While it is undoubtedly true that these revelatory experiences can occur anywhere, it also seems to be true that what we can loosely describe as systems or traditions of revelation have appeared in history and have become the predominant ways in which the experience of God is mediated. There can, however, be no external proof of the authenticity of these systems of revelation. All we can tell from outside is something about the surface event that surrounds the disclosure: where, when and what was claimed.

There is no system of verification from outside that will get us close to the truth that is revealed. The truth of the experience can only be discovered from within the experience: we can only see the light pouring in from outside once we are inside. This is why attempts to provide naturalistic or rationalistic explanations of essentially religious claims always miss the point, whether the motive is negative or positive. The historical event, the thing that is available to our investigation, however elusively, is never itself the revelation but only the bearer of it, and no amount of historical dissection will prove or disprove it. The revelation comes through the event but is not enclosed within it. The relationship is always living and dynamic, which is why these systems of revelation are still effective means of disclosure for those who find the right attitude towards them.

This is why the ancient fear of idolatry, of identifying the mystery revealed with the thing that reveals it, still has something to teach us, though we must immediately go on to recognize that as we are presently constituted we have no other means of access to the mystery, and it is inevitable that the means by which the revelation is made will become sacred to us by association: the bearers of the Holy will, in some sense, partake of the holiness they convey. The temptation to fundamentalize the means through which the revelations come, to make them material equivalents of the spiritual truth they bear, is inevitable but dangerous. On the level of day-to-day experience it probably does not greatly matter. The peasant woman who worships the consecrated host in the Christian Eucharist as God, or the evangelical university student who treats the words of the New Testament as the literal dictation of the Holy Spirit, are not in any danger as long as they do not draw false conclusions from their personal experiences. God is being disclosed to them, the universal is conveying itself through the particular, but it is idolatry to make them identical. The idolatry may not matter very much on the private level, but it is altogether different when it is raised to the level of theory, when the consecrated host or the words of scripture are offered as evidence of the reality of God. They cannot provide us with external, independent evidence of that reality, so they cannot be used to prove anything. Their truth is inside their structure, not outside. They only work as means of revelation when they are submitted to.

The argument is circular, of course, but, as Karl Barth pointed out, it is not a vicious circle. When we step into the circle of faith we see its truth from inside. The truth of God is self-attesting, self-authenticating. We cannot know it from outside, find any external attestation of its truth, either by analysing the consecrated host in a laboratory or by exhaustively verifying the historical accuracy of the events that convey revelatory truth. And the same principle holds against those who try to dismiss revelation by reducing the modes of revelation to a tiny historical residue. The triumphant conclusion from the laboratory that the bread of the eucharist is only bread after all does not get us anywhere in testing the claims of sacramental theology, and the sifting of the New Testament for kernels of hard historical fact about Jesus, while an interesting and useful exercise, does not help us to answer the primary question that is put to us by Jesus: "*Who do you say that I am?*" Presumably there was no purely historical problem for those who originally encountered Jesus: he was there in front of them and his words were in their ears. But, as we know, that proved nothing of itself. The claim Jesus made on the lives of others was never resolved on the external, historical level. The facts that confronted them were differently interpreted and are still interpreted differently. There is no independent, disinterested authority to which we can appeal for a judgement, on the basis of which we can reach a conclusion. The truth of the claim can only be discovered inside, at the price of a certain submission.

Some words that the critic Northrop Frye wrote capture the paradoxical nature of this truth and they apply to all revelatory systems. He wrote:

We are sometimes urged to "demythologize" the gospels in order to make them more relevant to modern canons of credibility. "Modern" in such contexts usually means about a hundred years out of date, but still an impulse to try to remove whatever seems obviously incredible is natural enough. It would be interesting to see, if we could, what the original "historical" Jesus was like, before his teachings got involved in the mythical and legendary distortions of his followers. But if we try to do this with any thoroughness, there will be, quite simply, nothing left of the gospels at all. The gospel writers, or editors, have been too clever for us, and whenever we think we have found something unique and "real", in historical terms, we also find that they have blocked up that exit too with some echo from or parallel with the Old Testament or contemporary Jewish ritual that suggests some other reason for its being there. And yet they do not seem to be clever men, in that sense: their aim is clearly to try to tell us something, not to prevent us from knowing something else. There is early secular evidence for the rise of Christianity, but there is practically no real evidence for the life of Jesus outside the New Testament, all the evidence for a major historical figure being hermetically sealed within it. But it seems clear also that the writers of the New Testament preferred it that way.[2]

Revelation, it seems, cannot be reduced to any other category, any more than we can convert music into words, or poetry into prose. We must submit to the medium if we would discover its truth.

The trouble is that the revelations that come to us are all mediated through human beings and their instruments. Some individuals may have direct experience of God, but when the rest of us want to assess what they have seen and heard it comes to us secondhand, through *them*, and the medium always affects the message. We have to be persuaded of their vision and we are resistant to persuasion for a good and for a bad reason.

Throughout history many false claims have been made about the nature of reality, so we have developed a filtering system to deal with them. Scepticism, as we have already noticed, is the filter, and we need it. There is a lot of spiritual and intellectual poison around and we must not let it into our system or it will damage us, so we filter it out. But absolute scepticism, a filter so thick that nothing will get through it, is just as deadly. We can be destroyed by our own scepticism, because we fail to open ourselves to the genuine truths that are important to our health. We have to admit that some people hardly filter out anything and they become religiously obese, taking in everything that comes to them, swallowing extraordinary and extravagant views, filling themselves with absolute certainty about everything under the sun and much that isn't. In anxious and foreboding times, such as the ones we live in, some people are strongly disposed to a kind of over-belief. They look for systems that will offer absolute guidance through the perplexity of history, and give them absolute guarantees of meaning and value. We see this search for absolute certainty in areas other than religion, politics being a potent example. The zealot or fundamentalist finds a teaching or theory that closes off the anguish of doubt and uncertainty, and removes the pain of freedom and personal responsibility. The resulting commitment can be absolute allegiance to an infallible institution or an infallible document that contains clear directions for living and a precise statement of the meaning of history. But this does not exhaust the attractions of absolutism. Of equal importance is the sense of belonging that such absolute commitment brings. The initiate is brought into a group of the enlightened who fortify each other with the compulsive and infectious power of the secret knowledge they share. The mystique of the secret society is one of the most potent things in history. It assuages loneliness and flatters our self-importance at the same time. This helps to account for the power of the sect in every generation, whether it is religious, political, literary or even theological. We see a resurgence of fundamentalist thinking throughout our world in these times, the most potent being the emergence of groups who combine religious and political absolutism, such as Islamic fundamentalism in the Middle East and Pro-testant fundamentalism in the United States of America.

This kind of over-belief is one danger in religion, but the opposite danger is just as grave and helps to prepare the soil for the rank growths it so despises. This is to become spiritually or morally anorexic, to become so resistant to revelation, to spiritual and moral truth, that we starve ourselves utterly of it. The prevailing intellectual tendency in the West has probably been in that direction in recent years. The fashion is to adopt a scepticism so thick that it is impervious to the subtle and poetic nature of spiritual truth. The difficulty here is that religion is a soft medium. Unlike certain sciences, it is difficult to come by irrefutable evidence in religion. We are dealing with the mystery and meaning of life and we face a double problem. It is not just a matter of doing what is right (hard enough when we know what it is); it is actually discovering what is right, knowing the truth, that is difficult. How are we to assess the competing claims, measure the exact force, of the data of religion? This material never comes to us with indisputable clarity. It is always mediated through individuals of genius whose lives are no longer directly accessible to us, and whose messages are invariably affected by the labours of their interpreters and the institutions that have developed around them. So the subject matter of religion becomes an obvious hunting-ground for absolute sceptics. Revelation is a frail medium that requires a kind of modesty and passivity from those who would open them-selves to it. If it is viewed simply as an inert mass of dead history it will never yield us anything, but if it is approached as a living reality it still has transformative and evalua-tive power. Before the disintegration of the structures that used to transmit the values and meanings of religion and morals, most people absorbed something of the great spiritual traditions through family, church, school and, from them, society. Today that great constellation of tradition-bearing structures has been eroded by the acid of a scepticism that has relativized value and seems to have burned out of many people the disposition that is sensitive to the delicate signals of transcendence.

It is not surprising, therefore, that many have reacted against the confusion of the times by rushing into systems that restore order and banish doubt. The paradox is, of course, that if we remove doubt we remove the need for faith, for faith is the decision we make to trust the truth of revelation even though no absolute proof is ever given to us. It is, in fact, faith itself that is under attack in these days, from the left and from the right, from those who tell us we can know nothing and from those who tell us they know everything. For those who try to choose the narrow way of faith, the middle way between absolute doubt and absolute certainty, the journey is not easy. We have to accept a large degree of uncertainty in the language we use about God and his mysteries. We have to accept that much of the way is hidden from us, and that the light we are given, while it is strong enough for our journey, is not bright enough to illumine all mysteries. Nevertheless, we choose to act on the knowledge we have received, to walk in the light we have been given, because if we wait till we know all, we shall wait for ever.

Revelation, then, is the heart of religion. Religion is the human response to revelation; it is what we have made of what has come to us from the mystery that besets us. It requires a delicate balance of responses from us, a sort of reverent scepticism or sceptical reverence. We are to confront a living tradition that mediates God, but the gift comes to us in earthen vessels and we have to learn to distinguish between the two, understanding that the vessel itself is due a kind of reverence, though it must never be absolute.

But what system of revelation are we to enter? We are faced with many traditions, and many sub-species within single traditions, and we clearly cannot enter them all. Students of religion may study many systems, but the study of religion is not the same thing as submission to religion. Opening ourselves to the revelatory power of a spiritual tradition requires commitment and time, and we are unlikely, in a single lifetime, to exhaust the possibilities offered by any one system. It is true that every system will be culturally and historically conditioned and expressed, but this is an inescapable fact. We can only experience marriage by being married to a single person and the reality of that person will inevitably colour and limit the experience, but there is no alternative. The experience of marriage is mediated in the particular, and so is the experience of religion. This has been called "the scandal of particularity" by one theologian. The word *scandal* in this context means something that offends or trips us up, and there is no doubt that a certain kind of mind is offended by the specific claims made by particular traditions.

The Christian tradition is a good example of this particular kind of offence. Its exponents have made claims for its uniqueness and finality in a way that causes deep offence to followers of other religions, as well as to those who think of themselves as open and fair-minded about the disputing claims of all religions. We must immediately concede that, on one side, these claims about uniqueness and finality are often examples of straightforward human egotism and pride, fortified by ignorance of other traditions. But something else can be said on the other side. When people enter a spiritual tradition it becomes for them a unique focus of revelation. For them it is final. God has come to them through it. We have already noticed the almost unavoidable tendency in human beings to fundamentalize the means through which they have discovered God and to build a false identity between them. This is why advanced practitioners of any spiritual discipline seek to move further and further away from forms and images, because they recognize that they can take the place of God and become absolutes in their own right. This happens in most spiritual traditions, but it is present with particularly insidious power in Christianity.

Christianity is the historical system that carries the particular revelation of God in Jesus Christ. Jesus Christ was undoubtedly unique, if only in the sense that he was a particular person in history, and Christianity is the means by which that uniqueness is mediated, but it is dangerous to claim uniqueness for *Christianity*, to create an absolute identity between the form of revelation and the content, which is God revealed through Christ. But there is undoubtedly a sense in which Christianity itself is the unique and final means of encounter with God for those who have entered it. It is possible, however, to affirm the unique nature of the experience for those who have entered it, without engaging in corresponding denials of other avenues of revelation about which we know little or nothing. Wesley Ariarajah captures this experience well. He writes:

> When my daughter tells me that I am the best daddy in the world, and there can be no other father like me, she is speaking the truth. For this comes out of her experience. She is honest about it; she knows no other person in the role of her father. The affirmation is part and parcel of her being . . . But of course it is not true in another sense. For one thing, I myself know friends who, I think, are better

fathers than I am. Even more importantly one should be
aware that in the next house is another little girl who also
thinks that her daddy is the best father in the whole world.
And she too is right . . . For here we are dealing not with
absolute truths, but with the language of faith and love . . .
The language of the Bible is also the language of faith.
Whether we are speaking about the chosen people, or about
Jesus as the only way, we are expressing a relationship that
has profound meaning and significance for us . . . The
problem begins when we take these confessions in the
language of faith and love and turn them into absolute
truths . . . Such claims to absolute truth lead only to intolerance and arrogance and to unwarranted condemnation of
each other's faith-perspectives.[3]

If we want to open ourselves to a system of revelation,
through which we can learn to apprehend the nature of
the mystery that surrounds us and the reality of our own
condition, then we must enter by one door, choose one
tradition and submit to it. And we can do this without
engaging in judgement on other ways, either negatively or
positively. Our energies and attentions are going to be fully
engaged, without expending them on wasteful comparisons
with other traditions.

There is, however, one other matter we ought to glance at
before proceeding with our exploration. I am a Christian and
it is the Christian way that I shall seek to describe in this
book. Christianity is an enormously rich spiritual tradition
that offers insights into the meaning of life and how to live
it, as well as containing a range of methods of prayer and
spiritual formation that have been tested down the centuries.
But all this richness and truth has been conveyed through
history in earthen vessels, and for some communities, as for
some individuals, the medium has hopelessly compromised
the message. Many individuals have been turned off Christianity for ever by the harsh, unyielding and unlovely religiosity of their parents or guardians. That is why it is important
for people who are exploring Christianity to make a fundamental distinction between the substance or content of the
Christian revelation and the form in which it is embodied.

We have seen that there is an inescapable tension here. As Paul told us, we have this treasure in earthen vessels, but we cannot successfully separate the two. Many attempts have been made in the past to evolve a pure Church in which the content of the message is perfectly reflected in the human and institutional instruments that bear it, but it is a vain search. Sooner or later the inescapable human element asserts itself and deforms the original vision. Individual Christians know this personally in their own experience. They may be caught by the vision of Christ and his purity, and seek to be true to it, but they are always having to wrestle against their own flesh and blood, and the struggle will last till the end of their lives. And this struggle is mirrored and heightened in the institutional or corporate aspect of Christianity. It is difficult enough for individual Christians to reflect the purity of Christ, but it is even more difficult for Christian groups to do so, because the institutional side of Christianity has its own dynamic, its own politics and rivalries. St Augustine of Hippo used the mysterious story in the Old Testament which describes Jacob's all-night wrestling match with the Angel of God at the Brook Jabbok, to express this theme. We are told that when dawn came and the angel left Jacob, he was wounded in his thigh and went off limping as the sun rose. Augustine sees Jacob, both blessed and wounded, as a true image of the Church.

> Look at this man: on one side he was "touched" by the angel with whom he wrestled, and that side shrank and was dried up; but on the other side he was blessed. It is the same man, one part of him shrunk and limping, and the other blessed and strong . . . The shrunken part of Jacob signifies the evil Christians, for in the same Jacob there is both blessing and limp. The Church of today still limps. One foot treads firmly, but the other drags. Look at the pagans, my brothers. From time to time they meet good Christians, who serve God. When they do, they are filled with admiration, they are attracted and they believe. At other times, they see evil-living Christians, and they say, "There, that is what Christians are like". But these evil-living Christians belong to the top of Jacob's thigh, which shrank after the

angel had touched it. The Lord's touch is the hand of the
Lord, straightening and giving life. And that is why one
side of Jacob is blessed, and the other shrunken.[4]

It is certainly true, as Augustine states, that there are evil
Christians and good Christians, but today we would be less
confident than Augustine in stating it in precisely those terms.
The division between good and evil is found within each
Christian and within every Christian institution. Each of us
is blessed and wounded, straight and shrunken, and the record
of Christianity reflects the abiding ambiguity.

The supreme paradigm of this confusion, as it affects the
institutional side of Christianity, is provided by the relationship between Christianity and the Jewish people. Jesus was a
Jew and his earliest followers were all Jews, but most of his
countrymen did not join the Christian movement. In A.D.
70, forty years after his death, Jerusalem was destroyed by
the Roman army and the Jews gradually spread throughout
the world, a race apart, always strangers, despised, mistrusted
and exploited. Something of the stubborn but exasperated
anguish they felt comes through in Shakespeare's famous but
unlovely play *The Merchant of Venice*, in Shylock's speech:

> Hath not a Jew eyes? Hath not a Jew hands, organs, dimen-
> sions, senses, affections, passions? Fed with the same food,
> hurt with the same weapons, subject to the same diseases,
> healed by the same means, warmed and cooled by the same
> winter and summer, as a Christian is? If you prick us, do
> we not bleed? If you tickle us, do we not laugh? If you
> poison us, do we not die?[5]

It is tragic to acknowledge that most of the Jewish per-
secutions have been whipped up by Christians. There were
innumerable massacres of Jews by Christians in the Middle
Ages. Edward I drove them out of England in the fourteenth
century. They were driven out of Spain, massacred in the
Holy Roman Empire, persecuted in France. They were
hunted and persecuted into this century, and it is our century
that tried what has been called "the final solution" to the
ancient problem of the Jews: systematic extermination. Six

million of them were killed by the Nazis in gas oven and firing ditch. A few individual Christians by their courage and compassion relieved the blackness of the picture with private acts of kindness and heroism, but the prevailing tone is of unmitigated night.

David Edwards has pointed out that the historical forces which were the immediate causes of the Holocaust had been preceded by centuries of Christian anti-semitism:

> In 1543 Martin Luther's tract on *The Jews and their Lies* echoed the vilest medieval propaganda. Foul libels, such as stories about child murder or cannibalism, had been very widely believed. Riots and massacres had been countenanced or commanded by Christian rulers. Jews had been forced into unpopular professions and had then been expelled penniless. And very few Christian consciences were troubled – for it was taught in church that the Jews were being justly punished for "killing God". The New Testament itself seemed to condemn the Jews. Passages of Paul's letters suggested that the Jewish religious law brought nothing but enslavement and misery, and in the gospels could be read heated attacks on Pharisees, priests and scribes. Most modern scholars attribute at least some of the fierceness of these attacks to the gospel-writers rather than to Jesus, remembering that the gospels were written in the very period when church and synagogue were being divorced. But Matthew 25 was a diatribe against Jewish "blind guides" who did everything for show, overlooked the demands of justice, mercy and good faith, were "brim-full of hypocrisy and crime", stopped men entering "the Kingdom of Heaven" and made converts who were "twice as fit for hell as you are yourselves". The same gospel reported the fateful Jewish cry: "His blood be on us, and on our children!" (Matthew 27:26). The fourth gospel was also used in anti-semitism. Although in that gospel Pilate is the only Gentile who speaks to Jesus, who declares that "It is from the Jews that salvation comes" (John 4:22), yet Jesus is condemned by Pilate in order to satisfy the Jews (John 19:16). "The Jews" – a phrase which occurs about seventy times – are told that "Your father is the devil and

you choose to carry out your father's desires" (John 8:44). All the Jews' teachers before Jesus were "thieves and robbers" (John 10:8). It is a history which must make all Christians with open hearts and minds profoundly ashamed, for it is clear that the Church's history and even the Church's gospels have been poisoned by the great evil of hatred for the religion and the race that gave Jesus birth, nourished his soul and supplied his audience. This history resulted in a Jewish tradition which until recently avoided even naming Jesus – and it still makes the idea of conversion to Christianity unthinkable for almost all Jews. "I am a Jew", said the religiously agnostic Isaac Deutscher, "by force of my unconditional solidarity with the persecuted and the exterminated."[6]

When in 1972 Pope Paul VI solemnly declared that the Jews were not guilty of the death of Jesus, his ungrudging declaration underlined the horrific nature of the Christian record. Anti-semitism is probably the most hideous blot on that record, but it is far from being the only one. When we have not had unbelievers to persecute we have turned upon each other, and when we have sometimes exhausted ourselves, we have often continued the war by other means. Christianity today is as well-known for its divisions as for its allegiance to Jesus Christ. On a recent count it was reckoned that there are in the world at least twenty thousand different Christian denominations. Christianity is flawed, and when we enter it we must enter it without illusions, remembering always to distinguish between the revelation and the instrument that bears it. Only a humble Christianity will commend itself today, and Christians have much to be humble about. But realism about human nature is part of the Christian message, and regular confession of sins is part of our discipline. As Psalm 103 has taught us, "We know whereof we are made; we remember that we are but dust", but Augustine also taught us that our dust has a glory prepared for it. Dust we are, but troubled dust, dust that dreams and struggles. Like Jacob we limp, but we are also like Jacob as we struggle towards the sunrise.

IV

THE WORD

One of the main difficulties presented by Christianity to anyone who wants to encounter it is the variety of forms in which it comes. We have already noticed that there are about twenty thousand separate versions of Christianity in the world today. Most of them have their origin as separate groups in dispute or disagreement with other versions of the Christian Faith, and it is the disputatious nature of Christian theology that we ought to look at next. The major divide in Twentieth-Century Christianity often runs through the separate denominations as well as between them, and it usually concerns the approach we are exhorted to take to the nature of the historical claims that are made about early Christian origins. The thing that makes Christianity so controversial is its dependence upon a specific historical focus. It is true that we will find a prophet or visionary of genius at the beginning of most of the great religious systems, but their impact is often abstracted into a generalized spirituality that has been effectively unlinked from the original revelational encounter. In Christianity the link between its message and its founder is essential to its meaning, but the way Christians understand that link varies enormously.

It is tempting to dismiss the differences between Christians as evidence of the kind of pathology that frequently accompanies the activities of any group of ideological protagonists. Human beings are peculiarly at the mercy of the fixed idea, the unconscious assumption and the hidden agenda, and these three elements enter and complicate debate on abstract topics that are beyond the reach of accurate verification. I once interviewed a well-known and extremely articulate atheist on a television programme. A few days later I received a letter from someone who claimed to be "a Bible Christian", challenging my guest to provide a scriptural basis for his point of

58

view. This is an extreme example of bondage to a fixed idea rendering its holder quite incapable of entering imaginatively into the mental world of another. Religious disputes are frequently dismaying to the listener because they are often dialogues between the deaf. It is not surprising that people of a temperate and sceptical nature often choose to avoid religious and political debate entirely, convinced of the intractable and irresolvable nature of the material under discussion. It certainly seems to be the case that what may be *known* in a solidly provable way in both areas is wildly disproportionate, in its slenderness, to the passion, conviction and sheer range of claims made by political and theological protagonists.

The difficulty arises because in both religion and politics the theoretical base, however fragile, supports a vast and complicated practical enterprise that has profound effects upon the actual lives of numberless individuals. The paradox is that areas as tangled and misty as religion and politics ought to call for gifts of caution, humility and patience in those who would guide us through them, yet there is something about their very existence that summons the very opposite characteristics, so that theological and political dispute is loud with the passionate claims of incompatible systems. Bertrand Russell once pointed out that people are zealous for a cause when they are not quite positive that it is true, and that is almost certainly the case here. In an area as imprecise as religion it is worth remembering something that Charles Williams said: *"No one can possibly do more than decide what to believe."* That decision need not be arbitrary or irrational, and it can be held with a firmness that is unto death, but it is unlikely to commend itself if it protests its certainties too much. People adopt religious positions for many reasons, but the heart of honest and effective religion lies deeper than argument, where the claim of Faith authenticates and attests itself in the soul of the believer. Herbert Butterfield, the historian, once exhorted Christians: "Hold to Jesus and for the rest be uncommitted." But it is precisely on what holding to Jesus involves that Christians disagree. My intention in this book is not polemical. I am not interested in opposing anyone's way of holding to Jesus, mainly because I believe that the real encounter with Faith takes place, as I have already suggested, on a level deeper than argument. Nevertheless, some way forward from the central issue that divides us is important.

The main problem that divides Christians today is the nature, status and use of the Bible, particularly the New Testament. The historical basis for their claims is very important to Christians. They claim to have encountered the mystery of God in the actual, historical specificity of a man of Galilee called Jesus of Nazareth, later called the Christ, from the Greek word for "anointed", because they also linked their claims about him to the ancient hope of the Jews that God would send them a redeemer king, the anointed one. So Christian claims are grounded in an actual human being, but the historical nature of the claims they make is elusive, and their appeal to history is ambiguous. It is obvious that it is not history as such that provides them with the ground of their faith, because many of those who knew Jesus in the flesh did not come to faith in him, though they were all too aware of his historical actuality. Even if we accept that there was a genuine revelation of God made through Jesus, we have already noted that revelations have to be acknowledged and accepted if they are to be effective. In effectual revelation there has to be an actual event or person that is the mode of the revelation, but the revelation can only be given or made to hearts and minds that are tuned to receive it. In other words, revelation is not universally and overwhelmingly self-evidencing. On the contrary, it seems by nature to be non-assertive, self-effacing, secret. In the scriptural accounts, the people who are most open to it are people who wait and watch, people who have spent time gazing into the mystery of things, looking off into the distance, trying to discern meaning. We might also guess that those who are to some extent uncertain about themselves in the order of things, not entirely in control or command, are more likely to be receptive to what comes to them from others; while the controlling and masterful, the ones who know exactly what is going on and why, are less likely to notice the modest and subtle disclosures of God, or of anyone else, for that matter. But whatever their reasons, we know that many of those who encountered Jesus saw only Mary's son, the carpenter, whose brothers and sisters they knew.

So the claims made about Jesus are not straightforward and they are not objectively verifiable. That is to say, he is not like a vast pillar in a remote desert whose fabled dimensions can be checked with a measuring tape, if only we can get to the place. Claims about Jesus are not like that, because what we bring to an encounter with him affects what we see and hear. This is certainly what happened in the pages of the New Testament. We see the action mainly through the eyes of the main characters among his disciples, those who committed themselves to him (although we know that his followers were varied in their estimation of him and fluid in their commitment), but there must have been many who encountered him on a variety of levels, whose lives he touched in some way, who yet remained puzzled about the exact nature of their relationship with him. We know that he healed many, that many heard him preach. He clearly was a man with a gift of sympathy, and many came to him for a word of compassion, reassurance or forgiveness. Yet others received the sharp edge of his tongue as he cut through their pretences, self-delusion and cruelty being the only human faults that provoked him to anger. Many must have caught sight of him striding through a village, or sharing food with his little band of followers under a tree or by the sea-shore. And there were many that saw him lashed through the streets of Jerusalem to the Place of the Skull where he was crucified. He was the same man throughout all those encounters, but he was very differently estimated.

Peter confessed that he was Messiah (Mark 8:29). The woman of Samaria who met him at Jacob's well in Sychar described him to her friends as a man who had told her all that she ever did (John 4:29). For Nicodemus, a scholarly member of the Jerusalem Establishment, he was a teacher come from God (John 3). To a man born blind who was impatient with doctrinal bickering, Jesus was the man who had restored his sight (John 9:25). To the high priest he was a rank blasphemer (Mark 14:64). To the hard-bitten centurion who was on duty at the crucifixion he was a genuine man of God (Mark 15:39). And to doubting Thomas he was divine (John 20:28).

None of these various estimates of the significance of Jesus can be demonstrated historically to the exclusion of any of the others. They are all part of the fabric of history, but there are no external sources available to us to prove or disprove them. We only have the New Testament, and it is as enigmatic and unassertive as the nature of revelation itself. Northrop Frye has already captured the enigma for us, when he said that the meaning of the Bible was found within its structure, not without. It is true that external sources and information can lend their support to the background suggested by the New Testament narrative, or can cast doubts upon the accuracy of some of the incidental claims we find there. This may strengthen or weaken our trust in the text, but it won't help us to resolve the fundamental challenge of Christ's nature and significance. Historians can help us a little in wrestling with the texts about Christ, in pointing to what they think are editorial heightenings or elaborations of original stories. They may point out that Matthew takes stories from Mark, almost certainly the first gospel, and touches them up. They may speculate about how small blocks of narrative, stories or parables, attract to themselves what may be loose sayings that seem to have little connection with the original incident, except by association. But they can offer no more than their private opinions on the status and significance of Jesus, exactly as did the people in the New Testament itself, who were so varied in their responses to him.

This is why we should bring to our interpretation of the New Testament a certain caution and reserve. What we make of the New Testament will probably say as much about ourselves as about the text we are studying with attempted impartiality. We should not be ashamed or afraid of the fact that we are subjective: we can be no other way. But recognition of the inevitability of this personal involvement in interpretation should make us modest in the universal claims we make on behalf of what we see. We are all limited and modified in our attitudes to scripture by personal and cultural factors. These influence what we see there, and there is very little we can do about that – we can only see from where we are placed – but we should be cautious about asserting that ours is the only way to see or that what *we* see is the only thing there is. The debate about miracles is a good illustration of the point.

The American New Testament scholar and expositer Walter Wink has pointed out that scholars are often as dogmatic about what could *not* have happened in the New Testament as fundamentalists have been about what *must* have happened. He points out, for example, that historians cannot say whether miracles actually happened or not. They are inaccessible to historical judgement, since such judgements can only be made on the basis of analogies, and miracles by definition have no or few analogies. He goes on:

> Historians still can demand that adequate warrants or evidence be produced for believing that something unusual has happened; they can demonstrate how legendary elements have infiltrated the account (*if* there are parallel versions in which they are missing; otherwise it is largely guesswork). They can provide invaluable checks on superstition by casting a critical eye on extraordinary claims that have a tendentious bent. But to go beyond this to dogmatic assertions that faith healing, or clairvoyance, or resuscitation of the dead is impossible, is to go beyond one's competence as a historian to the faith assertions of a person caught in the narrow confines of a particular world view – or what Paul Ricoeur has called "the available believable".[1]

His use of Paul Ricoeur's phrase "the available believable" is extremely useful and interesting. Wink writes:

> In the 1920s, books by critical scholars on the healing stories in the gospels tended to say something like this: "Faith healing is impossible, since it would violate the laws of nature. Therefore the healing narratives are legends developed to glorify Jesus as the Christ." At the same time these books were being written, however, psychosomatic medicine was coming into its own, so that by the forties and fifties we were getting books that said something like this: "Psychosomatic healing is possible; therefore Jesus could have healed psychosomatic illnesses. All other healings ascribed to him are legends developed to glorify Jesus as the Christ." Now we are getting the solid results of scientific studies on the placebo effect, faith healing, ESP,

and the powers of the mind, and what seemed "impossible" only five years ago is now regarded by increasing numbers of competent researchers as within the realm of possibility. What has happened here? We have received not one shred of new evidence from the first century. What has changed is our conception of what is possible, on analogy with contemporary experience. The "available believable" has shifted, and with it, historians' judgements.

We cannot be but children of our age. For this reason it would be far more honest for historians (and we are all historians when we approach these texts) to suspend judgements about what is possible and speak only within their competence.[2]

Now, what is "available" to people in their use of scripture varies enormously. Some people see the New Testament as the absolutely accurate transcript of a live video of the life of Jesus. At the other extreme are a group of radical scholars who have become convinced that it is not history at all but is, rather, an almost entirely artificial construction used by later followers of Jesus as a vehicle for promoting their own ideas, conflicts and prejudices. It is obvious, therefore, that people vary enormously in their assessment of the historical nature of the New Testament. The vexing thing about their disagreements is that there is no independent arbiter who can be brought in to gather external, independent evidence that will establish the facts beyond dispute.

The claims of the New Testament are always in dispute, just as the nature and status of Jesus were always in dispute in his day. It is true that on occasion an apparently independent scholar from outside the Christian Church will enter the fray and point out a few home truths to the protagonists. For instance, Geza Vermes, the distinguished Jewish scholar, has declared himself amazed at the level of scepticism many New Testament scholars bring to their work. In his book *Jesus The Jew* he claims, as a historian, that a plausible historical background to the gospels can be established that confirms many of the titles used about Jesus and some of the claims made about him. He cannot, of course, establish the truth about the transcendent status of Jesus, nor can he establish its fraudulence, but he does establish a broad, historical credibility for the New Testament narratives, inasmuch as they talk about Jesus the Jew, rather than Jesus the Son of God, an identity that cannot be established by historical method.

But how is the ordinary person who wishes to encounter the spiritual reality of Jesus to handle this complicated debate between rival groups of Christian students? It would obviously be preposterous to claim that only a lifetime of intense study and scholarly research can fit us for an encounter with the New Testament. The difficulty seems to lie in the fact that we want from this faith encounter what it cannot by nature give us – hard certainty. Fundamentalists want to put their trust in reliable documents, verbatim transcripts of ancient encounters: they want to be certain, so they claim historical certainty for the New Testament. Sceptical New Testament scholars also hate the vacuum of uncertainty, so they pare the texts down to a minimal list of "facts" they think they can establish. Neither group possesses what Keats called "Negative Capability": "that is when man is capable of being in uncertainties, Mysteries, doubts, without any irritable reaching after fact and reason!" In encountering Jesus we are brought into the area of uncertainties, mysteries, doubts, and we bring to the encounter the person we are, with all our limitations, knowing that not everything is available to us, because we have been formed by and through a particular culture and background.

When we come to the New Testament to encounter its uncertainties and mysteries, therefore, we have to bring ourselves as we are and deal with whatever is available to our use in the scriptures that are open before us. Since we are not, in this encounter, engaged in historical research but in spiritual exploration, in an adventure into a possible reality that transcends history, we can only move by going into whatever opens up for us. The suppositional premise of the exercise is that divine revelation is still a possible reality, and that by opening ourselves as far as we can to as much of the sacred narrative as possible, we create the conditions that may make that encounter a reality. As a matter of fact, this is exactly what happens in the actual way we use the New Testament, the difference being that many users usually go on to assert that their approach is the only legitimate one.

There are obviously, for instance, many people who read the New Testament in what we might call a literal way. They have no difficulty in accepting the miraculous elements in the narratives as descriptions of actual events, nor do they have the slightest qualm about accepting all the words that come from Jesus in the gospels as the virtual transcripts of his actual voice. But having done all that, they themselves have to go many stages further in their encounter with the text, if it is to be anything more than reading a history book. The religious use of the text, as opposed to its use as a historical source, involves a personal encounter with the one of whom it speaks at whatever level is available to us. A partial analogy may be provided by a violin, allegedly a Stradivarius. Scientific analysis may or may not answer the question of its origins: whether it is an absolute original, the brilliant product of a pupil close to the master, or a very much later piece of work, though faithful to the principles of the master in the carefulness of its craftsmanship. But the violin really exists to be played, not analysed; to provide an encounter with revelation, not an opportunity for scholarly disagreement. And the quality of the music teased from the violin will depend on the quality of the player and his or her commitment to the task. The person who is most convinced of its Stradivarian authenticity may not coax as much music from it as the more sceptical player, whose musical genius is higher.

That is why there have been many people in history who have adopted a more or less sceptical approach to the historical claims of the New Testament, who have, nevertheless, by their religious intensity and longing penetrated through the texts to a living and transforming relationship with the one of whom they speak. It is distracting and futile to try to force ourselves into an attitude towards scripture that we do not possess, mainly because we think it will be more religiously efficacious. We can only approach it as we are, with whatever level of credence or scepticism we have. There may be whole sections that are closed to us, unavailable to our use. That has to be accepted. We must use what is available, encountering Jesus as we can and not as we can't, but we must always remember that we are bound by our limitations, so we must not fundamentalize them and insist that others follow our approach. The other side of this modesty is that those of us who have little or no difficulty in accepting the authenticity of the narratives must not insist on truth tests for those who are more sceptical. Even blind Bartimaeus, who sat by the wayside, knew that something was going on when Jesus passed him by. He called out and was healed.

We come back here to the inevitable circularity that is the mark of all religion. It is a circle we must enter if we would discover its meaning, because it can only be tested from within. This is pre-eminently true of our use of scripture. Only those who have waited under it and used it patiently can testify to its extraordinary power. It is the testimony of millions that it is still a vehicle of revelation. It still has power to induce profound self-examination and to create the opportunity for that silence in which we are encountered by the mystery of God. That mystery of encounter takes place in a way that makes the historical status of the vehicle of revelation irrelevant. In the living use of the Bible the questions asked are always personal: What does this event mean in my life? Given that this is my attitude to the historical status of this particular incident, what is its truth for me at this moment? These are two of the questions we must ask ourselves.

And in asking ourselves these questions we are following the method Jesus adopted in his mission of disturbance and consolation. Jesus never taught abstractly or doctrinally. He told stories, grasped analogies and used encounters to sting people into awareness. The word used for this method is *parabolic*, from the Greek word for parabola or something thrown over something else, like a lasso. A parable uses a story or incident as a means of encounter with the truth. The story teller goes from living experience into hidden or ignored areas, and uses the known and familiar to disclose the unacknowledged or previously avoided. Stories take us from certainty and fact into "uncertainties, Mysteries, doubts". They shock or intrigue us into self-awareness and sensitivity, so that we become better disposed to encounter the transcendent reality whose absence haunts us.

In the second part of this book the parabolic or story

method will be used in an attempt to disclose the meaning of
Christ as revealed in his death. The intention is not to make
a case for abstract doctrine (though there is certainly a time
and need for that), but to provide the possible context for
some sort of personal response to the mystery of Christ. The
assumption behind the method used is that he is still one
whom we can encounter today, but that claim can never be
settled on general historical grounds, or as an established
universal truth. It is always a personal question, answered by
each person privately. The *world* does not know who he is –
but the individual may.

Part Two

ENCOUNTERING THE MYSTERY

He comes to us as One unknown, without a name, as of old, by the lake-side, He came to those men who knew Him not. He speaks to us the same word: "Follow thou me!" and sets us to the tasks which He has to fulfil for our time. He commands. And to those who obey Him, whether they be wise or simple, He will reveal Himself in the toils, the conflicts, the sufferings which they shall pass through in His fellowship, and, as an ineffable mystery, they shall learn in their own experience Who He is.

The Quest of the Historical Jesus,
Albert Schweitzer

V

GETHSEMANE

It is a quarter to midnight. You are on board ship in the South Atlantic, hundreds of miles from anywhere, cruising towards South America in a small cargo ship with a few passengers like yourself. You have dined well and spent the evening playing bridge with the other passengers. The captain informed you at dinner that at midnight the ship will cross another time zone and clocks will be advanced one hour. You finish your brandy and soda, and tell your bridge partners that you have decided to turn in for the night. You leave the lounge and make your way unsteadily to your cabin. The ship is rolling in a heavy sea and you have consumed a fair amount of alcohol. When you reach your cabin you suddenly decide to go up on deck and move your watch on one hour at midnight precisely.

Smiling to yourself at this sudden, rather whimsical decision you make your way to one of the lower decks, the ship rolling heavily. You lean over the rail and watch the waves pitching below you and the phosphorous wake of the ship, and at one minute to midnight you take off your watch and clumsily prepare to move it on one hour. But at midnight the ship suddenly dips into a trough and your watch slips from your fingers. You lean over the rail to catch it as the ship gives another mighty heave, and you find yourself going overboard into the water. There is no one near and no one sees you plunging into the sea. By the time you surface the ship is hundreds of yards away, the distance between you increasing every second. You panic and yell for help, but the ship moves inexorably away. "They will notice my absence and turn round", you pray, until you remember that you had said goodnight and gone to your cabin. No one will miss you until morning, and by then the ship will be more than a hundred miles away. You remember reading about other cases where men have fallen overboard and have remained calm, kept afloat and been rescued, so you try to swallow your panic and start swimming. You kick off your shoes and start swimming towards the lights of the ship that is now tiny against the horizon. It is intensely cold. You are alone in the sea, struggling to keep moving, trying to keep panic at bay. You swim, overwhelmed by images of your family, engulfed in loss and longing. You think of your fellow passengers, safely wrapped in blankets in their snug cabins. The sea crashes around you, vast and pitiless, and you cry out in your heart: "Out of the deep I cry unto thee, O Lord: Lord hear my voice."[1] Other flashes of the psalms rush into your mind:

> "Save me, O God: for the waters are come in, even unto my soul. I am come into deep waters, so that the floods run over me. I am weary of crying; my throat is dry: my sight faileth me for waiting so long upon my God."[2]

But there is no answer, no hand reaches down to pluck you out of the deep, no light from a rescue vessel cuts through the night towards you. You are utterly and finally alone, a tiny scrap of life, desperately trying to keep afloat on the face of the great deep, afraid even to think of the fathomless depth of the dark water below you. You are tiring rapidly now, slipping in and out of consciousness as you swim blindly onward, flashes of your life hitting the screen of your memory, engulfing you in regret and tenderness as the film rushes past. Will there be any consolation for you as you sink, any presence to steady you, or are you utterly alone, unnoticed and unregarded as you slip below the waves?

★

Now that may strike many of us as a rather extreme experience, but I offer it as a parable of human life, because it isolates the great question that life brings with it: are we radically alone in an indifferent universe in which we sink or swim, or is the universe friendly to us, does it care for us, even though its love may often seem to be mysteriously veiled? That is a question we may not care to think about, of course. It is a question that thrusts itself before us in extreme situations, but most people do not live as close to the edge as that. Most people are on board, after all, tucked up in bed or finishing off that game of bridge. The lights are on, the music plays, there are lots of people around: no need to think of the emptiness out there, the cruel sea, the loneliness, the hand slipping below the waves. But there are several reasons why we ought not to banish this question from our minds with a shiver, as we turn up the music and reach for the bottle to freshen up our drink.

In the first place, the anguish of a single person raises an enormous question against the universe; the anguish of a *single* person, yet history has never ceased to resound with the cry of Rachel weeping for her children, for they are not. There is in the centre of the Old Testament a plangent text called *The Lamentations of Jeremiah.* It is a great poem of suffering, a lament over the fall of Jerusalem and the destruction of the Temple, but it transcends that event and sings of all sorrow and all loss:

> How doth the city sit solitary, that was full of people!
> How is she become as a widow!
> She that was great among the nations, and princess among
>   the provinces,
> How is she become tributary![3]
>
> Is it nothing to you, all ye that pass by?
> Behold, and see if there be any sorrow like unto my sorrow,
>   which is done unto me,
> Wherewith the Lord hath afflicted me in the day of his fierce
>   anger.[4]

That is the voice of the hostage in Beirut, the voice of the young man dying of AIDS, the moan of the peasant starving in Africa, the cry of the wretched of the earth:

> A voice is heard in Ramah, lamentation and bitter weeping;
> Rachel weeping for her children refused to be comforted
> for her children, because they were not.[5]

These voices call us away from our own comfortable routines, however fleetingly, to contemplate sorrow and the meaning of sorrow. And even if we can ourselves find no meaning in it, we owe it to our unlucky brothers and sisters to sympathize with them in their affliction, to weep with those who weep.

But, there can be a delicious, almost guilty feeling of relief as we contemplate, however compassionately, the sufferings of others: so far our luck has held; we have not encountered the virus; we have always arrived safely on all our journeys; we are still on board and you won't find us hanging drunkenly over the rails; we intend to survive. That is why most of us will slow down and look curiously at the scene of a bad traffic accident, the body crumpled over the wheel, blood on the road, policemen already moving back the onlookers as the ambulances fight their way through. "Thank God it wasn't me, and it so easily could have been", we think, and a shiver of relief and premonition sweeps over us, as we ease back on the accelerator. We know we are always old enough to die, and at moments like that we hear footfalls on our own grave. We know, of course, that the statistics of life expectancy in our part of the world give us a long time yet, and then there is the ten year bonus added on by modern science and good behaviour, so we turn back to all that happy activity in the games room, but we have registered the fact that one day, even if we do not fall overboard, we'll be carried off, because no one travels for ever on this ship.

Whether we die bitterly and alone in the friendless dark or are carried off gently, die we shall, death being the one certain fact of our existence. And it is death that makes us ask what life means. If we went on living for ever there would be many problems to face, but life itself would not be one of them. It would spin along unconsciously in its endlessness, but because it doesn't, because it has a fixed boundary, it is a mystery to us and raises the question of its own meaning. It is limited and finite and therefore precious. There are people who end their own lives, but most people would choose to continue even a miserable life rather than end it. What is this mystery that surrounds us, this life with all its pleasure and pain, laughter and regret? We are thrown into it and then dragged away from it, looking back at it longingly as it recedes from our eyes, like a ship in the night from which we have been cast adrift. Even the very old leave it with regret, while the young are heartbroken.

Jesus died young, certainly by the standards of our expectations of life. There is a strong tradition in the New Testament that he foretold his own death. Mark quotes three occasions on which Jesus predicted not only the certainty of his death, but the manner in which he was to die. The first text comes in Chapter 8:31:

> And he began to teach them that the Son of man must suffer many things, and be rejected by the elders and the chief priests and the scribes, and be killed, and after three days rise again.

The second comes in Chapter 9:31:

> For he was teaching his disciples, saying to them, "The Son of man will be delivered into the hands of men, and they will kill him; and when he is killed, after three days he will rise."

And the third prophecy is found at Chapter 10:33:

> "Behold, we are going up to Jerusalem; and the Son of man will be delivered to the chief priests and scribes, and they will condemn him to death, and deliver him to the Gentiles."

Each of these prophecies was uttered while Jesus, with his disciples, was making his last journey up to Jerusalem. The progression in the tenses of the verbs is interesting and ought to be noted: The Son of man *must* suffer; later on, the Son of man *is* delivered into the hands of men; and finally, in Jerusalem, the Son of man *will be* delivered up. It is worth dwelling upon the significance of these apparently insignificant differences. First of all, the Son of man *must* suffer, it is necessary that he suffer, it is laid upon him by some compulsion, whether exterior or interior. Then a little later, the Son of man is delivered *now*, the necessity has overtaken him, he is already delivered over to his fate, and all this while he was still making his way to the Holy City before a hand had been laid upon him or an order sent out to arrest him. He cannot, at this stage, have been referring to the authorities in Jerusalem exclusively, because he had not yet been delivered up, handed over by them. It is true that an astute observer of the situation that had been created by the preaching and actions of Jesus might have predicted that it would all end in tragedy, but that is not the only thing he seems to be referring to. The necessity lies deeper than that. But who else other than the authorities in Jerusalem can be the agent of this necessity he feels? Who is handing him over, even now? The inescapable answer seems to be, God. The death of Jesus was not just a humanly contrived crime; it was, in some sense, also an act of God. God, Jesus seems to be saying, has decided upon, has seen the very necessity of my death. *"The Son of man must suffer."* He feels in his very depth that divine decision: it must be made. Later, he feels the decision has been made: the Son of man is delivered, the wheels are being set in motion, not by Caiaphas, Pilate or Herod, but by God. Only when that level of divine necessity has been established is there a prophecy of the human action that will soon follow: *"We are going up to Jerusalem and the Son of man* will be *handed over."* Taught by Jesus, the New Testament writers are convinced that the death of Jesus was the act of God as well as the action of men. The Acts of the Apostles calls it *"the determinate counsel and foreknowledge of God"*. At the very least that must mean that Jesus went to his death voluntarily, believing it to be his duty and calling to give up his life. As I have pointed out elsewhere:

None of this is intrinsically unlikely. We know from other episodes in human history that men of destiny frequently have premonitions of their own death, and even of the way it will come. The most obvious modern example is Martin Luther King, who was vividly aware of the likelihood that he would die at the hands of an assassin. On the night before he suffered he more or less prophesied his own death on the following day. These men, in fulfilling their destiny, unleash the forces of evil and opposition.[6]

Nevertheless, in spite of the voluntary element in his death and the sense he had that it was God's will, Mark tells us that Jesus prayed that the hour of his death might pass from him.

> And they went to a place which was called Gethsemane; and he said to his disciples, "Sit here, while I pray." And he took with him Peter and James and John, and began to be greatly distressed and troubled. And he said to them, "My soul is very sorrowful, even to death; remain here, and watch." And going a little further, he fell on the ground and prayed that, if it were possible, the hour might pass from him. And he said, "Abba, Father, all things are possible to thee; remove this cup from me; yet not what I will, but what thou wilt." And he came and found them sleeping, and he said to Peter, "Simon, are you asleep? Could you not watch one hour? Watch and pray that you may not enter into temptation; the spirit indeed is willing, but the flesh is weak." And again he went away and prayed, saying the same words.
>
> And again he came and found them sleeping, for their eyes were very heavy; and they did not know what to answer him. And he came the third time, and said to them, "Are you still sleeping and taking your rest? It is enough; the hour has come; the Son of man is betrayed into the hands of sinners. Rise, let us be going; see, my betrayer is at hand."[7]

We cannot tell what was in that prayer, but at that point most young men start bargaining desperately that the hour might pass from them. "There has to be a way out, a new drug they can try on me, someone who can heal me, someone who can get me out of here, because a great mistake has been made, I am not meant to be here, this cannot be happening." It is as though a great void were opening beneath us, like those awful nightmares we all get where we are falling and falling from a great height, and one day we wake up and we *are* falling, this time it is really true: the X-rays tell us, or the blood test, and the doctor suddenly seems a great way off – this is what it feels like, this is what Henry James called the distinguished thing, Death, the terminus.

It is a mistake, I believe, to think Jesus was without this fear of death, this engulfing regret, as he wrestled with God in the Garden of Gethsemane, sweating in anguish, so Luke tells us, with the sweat falling to the ground like drops of blood. Counselling the dying is a dreadful work, especially if they are young, because their plight is an offence. We agree with their sense of outrage and fear, but the fact that confronts them is inescapable, in spite of the devices they use to try to escape from it. Relief, of a sort, only comes after the moment of acceptance and surrender: "I *am* dying, going the way of all flesh, getting off the ship." Courage is the basis of all virtue, and it is courage that we need when the hour is come: courage, fortitude, the ability to take what comes without falling apart. Courage, of course, is not the false bravado that is weakness in masquerade. The courageous admit their fear, as Jesus admitted his: "*Father remove this cup; yet not what I will, but what thou wilt.*" The courageous are not ashamed to show their anguish, their fear, but they make of death a personal act, and many have redeemed their life by the manner of their leaving it.

The young man in the Garden of Gethsemane, whose hour had come, surrendered to it with courage: "*It is enough; the hour has come; see, my betrayer is at hand.*" We can sense the resolve after the struggle, the bargaining, the fear. The moment comes when we must look reality in the face, the reality of our own nature, the reality of what we have made of ourselves or unmade, the real thing behind the front, and the real death that has come for us, and embrace it. Jesus did. "*Rise, let us be going;*" he said, "*see, my betrayer is at hand.*"

Where did Jesus get the courage that enabled him to face the horrifying death he knew he would undergo? We have seen him wrestling in Gethsemane, and there must have been at least two elements in that inner conflict. First of all, was he right to be so confident in the convictions that were bringing him into conflict with the authorities? In situations of conflict, in the arena where power operates, whether it is power in ideas or power in politics, absolute conviction invariably ends in tragedy. We all have to learn to trade, to negotiate, to bend a little: no one has all the truth, so a little tactical compromise here and there is always wise; no one can be absolutely certain about everything, so a little modesty, a bit of flexibility makes sense. As the tempter said to Becket in *Murder in the Cathedral*: "*Be easy, man; it is the easy man who lives to eat the best dinners.*" Jesus was not an easy man, but we do not know what level of self-doubt there was in him about the collision course he was on. We know that he struggled with the nature of his vocation in the wilderness, testing his ideas, his motives, sifting them of self-interest, seeking to be true, and this is where it had led him. But had he been right, was there yet room for compromise, a deal with the authorities, a trade-off? This absolute conviction he felt, this closeness to the meaning of things, was it arrogance, self-delusion or was it the truth he had to die for? And added to that anguish of self-examination was the fear of death we have already thought about, the perfectly natural desire to cling to life a bit longer, to be here for another Spring, see the days draw in as the year ages, hear the geese flying south as the cycle of the seasons turns again. It is regret that makes cowards of us, sheer fondness for the things our eyes have seen and would see again and again. All this he wrestled with, alone, his disciples uncomprehendingly asleep. And he found the resolve, the high courage to go the way of absolute commitment.

But Luke tells us something else: "*And there appeared to him an angel from heaven, strengthening him.*" When we speculated about the last moments of that man adrift in the South Atlantic, we asked if there would be any consolation for him at the last, any sense of a presence beside him, gathering him towards his end. That is the biggest question life brings. We are beset by mysteries; we are thrown into life, and life does not seem to bear its own meaning. Are we alone in the universe or is there someone to whom we belong, to whom we return? Or do we cease at death, return to nothing? That is the question that comes with consciousness. And how are we to answer it? The reality of the physical universe is available to our senses and we can examine it, if only by means of mathematical calculations and radio telescopes, but that other possible reality, how are we to find it, know it is there or conclude that it isn't?

Jesus was one of that extraordinary group of people in history for whom that other supposed reality was more real than the physical universe and its heart-breaking joys and pleasures. We can apply to him what the Letter to the Hebrews says of Moses: *"He endured as seeing him who is invisible."* For Jesus, the invisible, the mystery that encompasses and tantalizes us, was personal, real and strengthening. It was from the unseen that he received strength; it was from the mystery that he found courage; it was from the invisible that he found the motive to surrender the consolations of the visible. It was the central reality of his life; he turned aside to have communion with it repeatedly; and it was the standard against which he measured life in the visible world. Does it exist? That is the question we address to the mystery that surrounds us. Are we alone in the universe, in spite of the courage of people like Jesus who die for what we think may be an illusion, or is there a presence in the mystery, a presence so powerful and so strange that knowledge of it reverses our standards, our instincts, our desires and longings, so that what we once clung to loses its power over us and what we once feared becomes our friend? How do we decide that issue? On what basis do we choose?

Millions of words have been spilled on this question and I have read and pondered many of them, but I have come to believe that the words can be a trap for us and we must learn to leap over them. There is no way we can settle the religious question from outside. There are no arguments, no reasons, no forms of words that can get us smoothly to the right conclusion. In chapter three I tried to explain this point by means of a parable based on my walks to Wytham Church. If we come across a country church while we are out walking we see the stained glass windows from outside as dull, opaque, closed-in on themselves. We cannot tell what they mean from outside. As long as we stay on the outside trying to figure out the design on the window, willing the mystery to turn itself inside out so that we can decide whether it is worth entering, we shall remain baffled for ever. But if we enter we see that the light pouring through the windows from the outside brings them to life, and we see patterns and pictures; through light we see light.

The essence of all religion is what we call revelation or illumination. There is a certain modesty about religious traditions at their best. They do not offer people clever arguments that explain the mystery of life, or conclusive proofs that settle all disputes. They say, quietly, "Come in and see, enter and sit awhile. The mystery is not at our command, we do not understand it (though we often try to control it), but we have seen and we know that light enters the universe, the mystery is uncovered. We cannot explain it to you or even describe it very well, but if you will cross the threshold it will explain itself, it will show itself, but only if you learn to wait, learn to sit still." The meaning of the mystery we encounter in religion cannot be known from outside itself; there is no way we can get it to explain itself to us from outside itself. There are no verbal equivalents of the mystery Faith experiences; there is no continuous line of argument which, if we are clever enough to follow it, will lead us ineluctably and irresistibly to the divine conclusion. We have to submit, submit just enough to bow our heads and enter the enclosure of faith. We may walk past, of course, many do, but the mystery will continue to trouble us.

> Footfalls echo in the memory
> Down the passage which we did not take
> Towards the door we never opened
> Into the rose-garden.[8]

And it is easy to understand why we are reluctant to go down that passage and open that door. Our difficulty is a cruel one: if there is no presence in the mystery that surrounds us, no God to comfort and receive us and give life meaning, then we need to find consolation somewhere else, and we can only look for it in this world, in this life, in what lies at hand. And there is plenty to console or preoccupy us, for a time. It is possible to give these consolations harsh names, and the harshness comes, I suppose, from disappointment, from those who have tried them and found them, in the long run, false comforters; but we should try not to give them harsh names because "any comfort serves in a whirlwind", as Hopkins reminded us, and if there is nothing out there, who can blame us for seeking to console ourselves? Frank Sinatra said he believed in anything that helped him through the night, and many of us have operated on a similar philosophy. Many things have helped for a time: making ourselves comfortable in this world by gathering a few riches; finding consolation in friendship or love, seeking solace in sex; taking the edge off life with drink or drugs or too much food; removing self-doubt with success and ambition – "making it". All of this has the power to charm and occupy our attention, and it fixes us firmly in this life. Our dilemma is that these things have the power to console us in the face of the emptiness that surrounds us, but at the possible cost of failing to encounter the mystery that may dwell in the emptiness. Our difficulty lies in finding the courage that will enable us to discover that presence, by learning to abandon some of the things that console us in its absence. What if there is nothing there? How can we make this commitment that may ask so much of us, without being offered irrefutable proof? Unless we can plunge our hands into the very side of God we will not believe. And it is here that the world-denying, death-defying courage of Christ may make us whimper with anxiety.

We are afraid of that great emptiness, the darkness that may or may not be alive with the presence of God, so we cling to the lights, the music and the happy company as we cruise through life, keeping away from the rail, shivering as we look at the sea through our porthole. And there is Jesus, as fond as we are of life, with more love for his family and friends, with a poet's eye for the fragile beauty of earth, abandoning it all for the sake of the unseen mystery, launching himself into the deep we dread. *"He endured as seeing him who is invisible."* That's what makes us whimper with fear and half-belief. It is one thing to be defiantly unbelieving, to know that the sea is empty, that we die alone, for then Jesus and those like him are magnificently mistaken, they are heroic suicides, throwing away the only life there is. But for those of us who are half-believers, inoculated with just enough

Christianity to prevent us catching it seriously, the courage of Jesus is an accusing sword through our hearts. His absolute commitment to the mystery, his passionate obedience to an invisible reality whose shape we cannot even guess at, fills us with both shame and longing.

For we have felt the twinge of absolute surrender; we have occasionally felt it rise in us as a longing for the kind of courage and detachment that gives up everything for the joy that is set before it; we have been drawn to the dazzling darkness and mystery of God and have thought to abandon ourselves to it, knowing at our heart's core that in that absolute loss we would find absolute consolation; but we have pulled back from it, afraid, back to the comforting chatter of the saloon, the whist and the brandy and the high laughter, while footfalls echo in the memory. So the longing jostles with shame as we watch others who seem to see what we long to see. This is why holy people – the truly surrendered ones for whom the world has become trivial – trouble and fascinate us. We are like the rich young man who came to Jesus because he was fascinated by his holiness, his freedom from all the things to which he himself was bound. Jesus loved him, and clearly saw the longing in him, the struggle to forsake all and follow him, yet the young man turned back sorrowful, torn in two.

> And as he was setting out on his journey, a man ran up and knelt before him, and asked him, "Good Teacher, what must I do to inherit eternal life?"
>
> And Jesus said to him, "Why do you call me good? No one is good but God alone. You know the commandments: 'Do not kill, Do not commit adultery, Do not steal, Do not bear false witness, Do not defraud, Honour your father and mother.'" And he said to him, "Teacher, all these I have observed from my youth." And Jesus looking upon him loved him, and said to him, "You lack one thing; go, sell what you have, and give it to the poor, and you will have treasure in heaven; and come, follow me." At that saying his countenance fell, and he went away sorrowful; for he had great possessions.[9]

Attracted as he was to Jesus he heard other voices in his ears, like the voices St Augustine heard as he wrestled with the mystery:

> Dost thou cast us off? and from that moment shall we no more be with thee for ever? and from that moment shall not this or that be lawful for thee for ever?[10]

How can we cast them off? We need them, they console us. Console us for what? For not knowing God. And how can we know God? By casting off the things that console us in the absence of God. But where are we to find the courage to do this, the faith to take this leap? I wish I could answer confidently as one who had found the courage and made the leap, but I can only answer as one who wants the courage and longs to make the leap. And again and again I come back to Jesus, the man of frighteningly absolute commitment, who spared not himself, yet looked with love upon the rich young man who turned and went away sorrowful. If there is any way of encountering the mystery it is in Jesus, because his commitment to the invisible mystery is so absolute that he is one with it, so that we say that in him the invisible became visible. This is partly what we mean when we say that Jesus is divine; his surrender to God was so absolute that his will became utterly conformed to the divine will, even unto death. In us everything gets complicated and mixed up; in Jesus there was clarity, clearness, purity of intention. In his light we see light. In him we discern the invisible mystery of the everlasting God.

As we sit and look at Jesus setting himself to make the final surrender of his will to God, we will encounter the mystery that haunts us and towards which we are afraid to go; and we may at last find the courage rising in us. But even if we do not find that, we may discover that he understands why we hang back, why our hearts are so often afraid. We may even find out that in God's heart there is room for the cowardly and uncertain. But first we must learn to sit still, learn to wait and watch the unfolding of the mystery hidden at the heart of Christ's Passion.

VI

JERUSALEM

It is very late in the evening, past bedtime, when you open the door of your room and look out into the corridor. The conference is being held in a small country hotel, and most of the participants are sleeping in rooms on this floor of the building. You are one of the main speakers at the conference, and at the introductory session after dinner you were introduced to the other participants. Praise was lavished upon you by the rather gushing chairwoman, and you had shifted with embarrassment as the other people at the conference looked at you with respect and expectation, all eagerly looking forward to your contribution and guidance on the following days of the weekend. But now they have all gone to their rooms and you are hesitating quietly as you look into the empty corridor. You tiptoe across the corridor to the door opposite, give one last look round, and then press your eye to the keyhole.

Suddenly another door in the corridor opens, just along from yours on the opposite side to where you crouch, now trembling with shame and confusion. The light from the opened door angles over you, and you can feel the presence of the person standing there gazing at you. You want to cry out, "No. It isn't that. You see . . . let me explain . . . you don't understand . . ." And the door closes quietly and you hear the person retreat into the room. Someone has found you out! You do not know who it is or how far the story will go, but someone at the conference has found out about you, and the knowledge has a shattering effect. You feel enormous shame, a desire to justify yourself and the conviction that it will be impossible to do so. You don't know who the observer was and you would find it impossible to explain, anyway, to come out of it all with your self-image intact, your reputation what it was.

"Reputation, reputation, reputation! O! I have lost my reputation. I have lost the immortal part of myself, and what remains is bestial. My reputation, Iago, my reputation!"[1]

Shame is a frightful thing to live with: to feel the accusing eyes of others upon you, assessing you, judging you, knowing your secret, your flaw, gazing at your hidden wound. The theme varies enormously in human history, but the burden of shame is constant. It leads some to suicide, some to compulsive and pathetic attempts to justify themselves, somehow wipe it all away with a flood of explanation. And round and round it goes, like the pain in the side of a chronically ill person who can find no comfortable position to lie in. Shame is the banner headline that strips away the pretence of your life and exposes you to the world. Found out at last!

Many people are found out in one way or another in life. Even more impressive is the fact that many people go through life afraid they'll be found out, afraid that the veneer will be stripped away and that they will be revealed in their true state. An article in the *New York Times* put an interesting modern gloss upon this phenomenon. The article was about Dr Joan Harvey's psychological research on the sense many people have that they are fakes. A friend of mine at Harvard preached a sermon based on the article and these are his words:

Dr Harvey was among several psychologists and therapists whose findings led them to conclude that many achievers feel they are fakes and impostors and live in terror of being exposed as the frauds they really are. The article discusses case after case of very bright high achievers in all fields who suffer from fear that others would discover their own sense of low self-esteem. This is called "the impostor phenomenon": no matter how secure you may appear to be, and no matter how high and successful you are, or even how lowly and modest you are, at heart most of us have moments of extreme anxiety about our real place in the scheme of things, and the characteristic nature of this anxiety is secrecy. Dr Harvey feels that the sense of fraudulence is so fundamental, so basic, that most people assume it is the natural state of things and would never think to discuss it or acknowledge it; thus, like some psychic cancer, it gnaws at our vitals, and the only release is death.[2]

The important thing to notice about this phenomenon is that it is a generalized feeling. Many of us, perhaps most of us, have specific things about ourselves we would be profoundly ashamed to have known or found out, but there also seems to be widely present a sense that we are somehow in the wrong, that we are hiding or putting up a front, faking it. Most of us cope with it, often by not acknowledging its presence or by burying it deep, but many cannot cope at all with their damaged sense of themselves, their low self-esteem, and they begin to act in self-destructive ways, or they behave grandiosely, acting a super self-confidence they do not feel. Others plunge into depression, often to the point of suicide.

But even if we are spared all this, are never found out, have no fear of being found out, are convinced there is nothing to find out, we are not excused our share in human misery. There is a discontent in all of us that sometimes acts like a permanent low level virus and at other times erupts into specific actions that can wreck our happiness. At its most amiable and bitter-sweet level it is illustrated in a cartoon I saw years ago of two newly-wed couples dancing. Each partner is being held closely by the other, but the man in one couple is gazing over the shoulder of his wife into the eyes of the other man's wife, who is hungrily returning the look. Discontent, inability to settle for what we have, even when we know how fortunate we are, is an abiding theme in human life. It gnaws at us all, but some of us break out and destroy the balance of our lives by reaching for what we cannot honestly possess. It is a theme endlessly rehearsed in literature and in classic legend, and the Bible is full of examples: David lusting in the moonlight for the wife of Uriah the Hittite is the most eloquent example of the human tendency to destroy our own happiness. The Bible does not theorize about the phenomenon, it simply describes it, holds up a mirror to it. Even the story of Adam and Eve is not a theory. It is a narrative that is meant to reflect the human capacity for tragic self-destruction and self-exile from happiness, from Eden.

Now the serpent was more subtle than any other wild creature that the Lord God had made. He said to the woman, "Did God say 'You shall not eat of any tree of the garden'?"

And the woman said to the serpent, "We may eat of the fruit of the trees of the garden; but God said, 'You shall not eat of the fruit of the tree which is in the midst of the garden, neither shall you touch it, lest you die'."

But the serpent said to the woman, "You will not die. For God knows that when you eat of it your eyes will be opened, and you will be like God, knowing good and evil." So when the woman saw that the tree was good for food, and that it was a delight to the eyes, and that the tree was to be desired to make one wise, she took of its fruit and ate; and she also gave some to her husband, and he ate.

Then the eyes of both were opened, and they knew that they were naked; and they sewed fig leaves together and made themselves aprons.

And they heard the sound of the Lord God walking in the garden in the cool of the day, and the man and his wife hid themselves from the presence of the Lord God among the trees of the garden. But the Lord God called to the man, and said to him, "Where are you?" And he said, "I heard the sound of thee in the garden, and I was afraid, because I was naked; and I hid myself." He said, "Who told you that you were naked? Have you eaten of the tree of which I commanded you not to eat?" The man said, "The woman whom thou gavest to be with me, she gave me fruit of the tree, and I ate." Then the Lord God said to the woman, "What is this that you have done?" The woman said, "The serpent beguiled me, and I ate." The Lord God said to the serpent, "Because you have done this, cursed are you above all cattle, and above all wild animals; upon your belly you shall go, and dust you shall eat all the days of your life."

Therefore the Lord God sent him forth from the garden of Eden.[3]

The Old Testament looks steadily at this phenomenon and reports it: Cain murdering Abel; Jacob defrauding Esau; the tragic insecurity of King Saul; the flawed greatness of King

David; the cupidity of King Ahab, who cannot rest until he has stolen from a small farmer called Naboth the vineyard of his ancestors.

And on it goes, but the most poignant example from scripture of the frailty of human nature is the account of Peter's denial of his Lord.

"Simon, Simon, behold, Satan demanded to have you, that he might sift you like wheat, but I have prayed for you that your faith may not fail; and when you have turned again, strengthen your brethren." And he said to him, "Lord, I am ready to go with you to prison and to death." He said, "I tell you, Peter, the cock will not crow this day, until you three times deny that you know me."

Then they seized him and led him away, bringing him into the high priest's house. Peter followed at a distance; and when they had kindled a fire in the middle of the courtyard and sat down together, Peter sat among them. Then a maid, seeing him as he sat in the light and gazing at him, said, "This man also was with him". But he denied it, saying, "Woman, I do not know him". And a little later someone else saw him and said, "You also are one of them". But Peter said, "Man, I am not". After an interval of about an hour still another insisted, saying, "Certainly this man also was with him; for he is a Galilean". But Peter said, "Man, I do not know what you are saying". And immediately, while he was still speaking, the cock crowed. And the Lord turned and looked at Peter. And Peter remembered the words of the Lord, how he had said to him, "Before the cock crows today, you will deny me three times". And he went out and wept bitterly.[4]

The most moving, truthful and perplexing part of this story is Peter's obvious love for Jesus, his pride in him, worship of him. Peter adored Jesus, and meant it when he said he would die for him, the way we always mean those vows we take in moments of high emotion and dedication.

Lay your sleeping head, my love,
Human on my faithless arm . . .

as W. H. Auden put it. As he denied Jesus, Peter loved him, as a man can love the wife he is unfaithful to, or the friend whom he has just slandered. We are creatures in conflict with ourselves, traitors to our own true loves, destroyers of our own peace. What is this enemy within us that constantly betrays us? Self-hatred, low self-esteem, insecurity and lack of trust lie at the bottom of it; all the complexes that are rolled into that much mistaken little word *sin*.

Many people assume that sin is a straightforward matter to deal with. It is, they claim, just a matter of not giving in, of pulling ourselves together, of avoiding what is wrong and doing what is right. But sin is a more profound mystery than that brisk attitude recognizes. We must not think that Peter did not know all that as he tore his own heart out of his chest and threw it away in that cold courtyard at dawn, long ago. He knew how despicable his behaviour was, he knew what a rotten, lousy thing it was, not only to desert your friend when all turn against him, but to deny that you ever knew him – Peter knew that, knew what he was doing, hated himself as he did it, knew it would break his heart and shatter his pride, even as he did it, said it, screamed it out: "Woman, I do not know him." To tell Peter to pull himself together, to snap out of it, to act like a man, is to tell the sun to shine at midnight in December. Peter wept because he knew the worst against himself better than anyone else; and he wept because he still loved Jesus; but above all, he wept because he knew that Jesus still loved him.

The complex profundity of human sin is best summed up for me in a number of women I have known whose lives were shattered at an early age because they were sexually abused by their fathers over a period of many years. There seems to be hardly anything that can heal a wound like that. The women all had a complex attitude to the experience: abiding shame and self-loathing; a sense of powerless complicity; a wildly fluctuating hatred for their fathers, to whom they were inexorably bound by blood and history. Several of the women became compulsively promiscuous, proving constantly to themselves their own guilt and responsibility for the early experiences, which had all happened in silence, at dead of night, in a sort of hideous slow-motion. They acted out their self-hatred by offering themselves to men, loathing them but seeking both affirmation and humiliation from them. They had often been dismissed as tramps, loose women without morals or pride, yet inside they were frightened little girls overwhelmed by a horror from which they could never escape.

This is an extreme example, but all sin has something of this nature, something baleful and self-directing that steals our joy from us, robs us of peace, holds us bound. In beginning to deal with it, we must first recognize it in ourselves, see how it is working, as we look with sympathy upon what we do to ourselves and those whom we love. But as we look in self-examination we must look with eyes not of judgement but of compassion. We have to look upon ourselves as Jesus looked upon Peter.

There are many examples of human sinfulness in the Bible, but scripture does not really give us an explanation for it. Indeed, any so-called explanation does not really succeed in doing more than describing the fact of sinfulness, and all the different ways of describing it do not really account for it. If we ask *why* a man eats too much we may say, "because he is just greedy"; but being greedy is doing anything to excess, so we have gone in a circle. Even if we use a more modern approach, and say that he may be eating too much because he is lonely or dislikes himself, we have not really explained *why* some lonely men, with low self-esteem, eat to excess; we have simply observed that they often do, and we also know from observation that some lonely men with a poor opinion of themselves eat like sparrows.

Part of the problem is that we like to find causes for things. A cause is a kind of pressure that effects something. The best example is provided by a row of dominoes. Push the first one and it hits the second, which hits the third and so on until they are all down. Every effect must have a cause, we say, every falling domino must have been hit by the one beside it. But someone has to start the process off, and in the case of sin it is difficult to explain how the first domino fell. In the story of Adam and Eve, for example, Adam blamed Eve and Eve blamed the serpent, but what got into the serpent? That bit is left hazy, but there are hints that the thing started in the spiritual realm, in some primal act of disobedience, some desire on the part of God's angels to be equal with God.

> Now war arose in heaven, Michael and his angels fighting against the dragon; and the dragon and his angels fought, but they were defeated and there was no longer any place for them in heaven. And the great dragon was thrown down, that ancient serpent, who is called the Devil and Satan, the deceiver of the whole world – he was thrown down to the earth, and his angels were thrown down with him.[5]

But what got into the angels? We cannot tell, nor can we offer a satisfactory account of human rebellion and irrationality. We are left with something that is simply there, part of the given situation and, therefore, a hunting-ground for theorists. However it got there, we are left with the observation that there is an intrinsic flaw in human nature, a disposition to irrational and self-destructive behaviour. And it magnifies in human history into social and political evil and personal misery. It spreads everywhere, infecting all our communities, even the most loving. It afflicts families, religious communities, congregations, nations and continents, seeping in everywhere, vitiating our vows, gnawing at the most tender bonds of kinship and friendship. It can be seen everywhere, the one constant of the human condition. It is behind every row in every backstreet, every car bomb in Beirut. It dominates our lives and we seek endlessly to moderate its effects; and there are always some in every generation who think they know how to eradicate it from the human condition. Whatever it is, whether we define it as a structural flaw or as the inevitable consequence of a human consciousness that is still evolving, it seems to be rooted in our spiritual and intellectual nature and it affects everything we touch. Milton probably said it best, in words he put into the proud mouth of Satan:

> The mind is its own place, and in itself
> Can make a Heav'n of Hell, a Hell of Heav'n.[6]

The drama of the story of Jesus is that we observe the effect he had upon the fallen human race, represented by the

characters who people the gospels. Jesus was the uncompro-
mised man, the pure man, the man uncomplicated by this
warp in humanity, and his effect was devastating, and still is.
In all his encounters we see the puzzled reaction of the flawed
to one who was sound and simple in essence. We see this
puzzled encounter between Jesus and the powers of this fallen
world at its most dramatic in the trial scenes before his
execution. In a sense, each of the characters in these scenes
represents one answer to human sinfulness, encountering
Jesus, the man in whom there was no shadow, no hidden
agenda. We see something of the impact of Jesus upon a
politician, upon religious leaders and upon visionaries and
idealists. The name of the politician was Pilate.

> When morning came, all the chief priests and the elders
> of the people took counsel against Jesus to put him to
> death.
> Now Jesus stood before the governor; and the governor
> asked him, "Are you the King of the Jews?" Jesus said,
> "You have said so". But when he was accused by the chief
> priests and elders, he made no answer. Then Pilate said to
> him, "Do you not hear how many things they testify against
> you?" But he gave him no answer, not even to a single
> charge; so that the governor wondered greatly.
> So when Pilate saw that he was gaining nothing, but
> rather that a riot was beginning, he took water and washed
> his hands before the crowd saying, "I am innocent of this
> man's blood; see to it yourselves".
> Then he released for them Barabbas, and having scourged
> Jesus, delivered him to be crucified.[7]

Pilate is a very familiar type in human history. He is the
realistic politician, world-weary and cynical, committed only
to containing and controlling the anarchic impulses of human
nature. People like Pilate are not necessarily indifferent to
morality; they may even prefer it where it will work just as
well as immorality; but they are mainly interested in keeping
things under control, because they despise the disorderly
passions of the multitude. Men like this, and they are usually
men, are often ascetic and controlled in their private lives,

their main lust being power; and they see their task as keeping the barbarians from the gates. Their attitude is sometimes described as the politics of original sin. They are usually unimpressed by theory or vision, having a very low opinion of human nature's capacity for righteousness. "What is truth?" Pilate said with weary mockery to Jesus in John's account of the trial. There is no truth, there is nothing that is absolute, no vision that is not hypocrisy, and those who speak in high-flown rhetoric are only gilding their own lust for power, their own sense of moral superiority.

Pilate clearly respected Jesus, in a sardonic way. Cynics are often intrigued by saints, because they are a contradiction of their own conviction that everyone is out for self-interest. Fortunately for the cynic's peace of mind, there are always very few saints around. What is perhaps more surprising is that Jesus seemed to have a compassionate respect for Pilate. He seemed to recognize the type, and to know the pressures he was under. He seemed to acknowledge that in this imperfect world there have to be people who manage things, keep things partially under control, and their managerial preoccupations limit their vision. The people the managers of the universe find most difficult are obsessional zealots who do not have the faintest understanding of what is possible and how things work. Pilate probably expected Jesus to be like that, but found in him none of that high-octane anger that character-izes the zealot, none of that lofty contempt for the unen-lightened that is their hallmark. Jesus did not say much to Pilate, but what he did say suggested a profound under-standing of Pilate's predicament: "*You would have no power over me unless it were given you from above*" (John 19:11), Jesus said to him, acknowledging the importance of the exercise of power, the techniques of management, in the world as it is.

It is characteristic that Pilate did try to release Jesus but then, when he realized that it would be imprudent and would probably lead to a riot, handed him over to death. His conscience would be well under control, of course. Jesus was just another piece on the board, but he had intrigued him. That night at the club during his first glass of claret he probably mused about him: "Odd chap that Galilean. Looked you straight in the eye, unlike that shifty bunch at the Temple. Pity there was no way I could get him off, a great pity . ., I say, waiter, bring me the menu please."

The other man in the deal patched up by Pilate was called Barabbas, and it is likely that he was one of the leaders of the movement for the liberation of Judea, a zealot. The zealots derived their name from the rather unpleasant story of Phinehas in the Book of Numbers:

While Israel dwelt in Shittim the people began to play the harlot with the daughters of Moab. These invited the people to the sacrifices of their gods, and the people ate and bowed down to their gods. So Israel yoked himself to Baal of Peor. And the anger of the Lord was kindled against Israel; and the Lord said to Moses, "Take all the chiefs of the people, and hang them in the sun before the Lord, that the fierce anger of the Lord may turn away from Israel." And Moses said to the judges of Israel, "Every one of you slay his men who have yoked themselves to Baal of Peor."

And behold, one of the people of Israel came and brought a Midianite woman to his family, in the sight of Moses and in the sight of the whole congregation of the people of Israel, while they were weeping at the door of the tent of meeting. When Phinehas the son of Eleazar, son of Aaron the priest, saw it, he rose and left the congregation, and took a spear in his hand and went after the man of Israel into the inner room, and pierced both of them, the man of Israel and the woman, through her body. Thus the plague was stayed from the people of Israel. Nevertheless those that died by the plague were twenty-four thousand.

And the Lord said to Moses, "Phinehas the son of Eleazar, son of Aaron the priest, has turned back my wrath from the people of Israel, in that he was jealous with my jealousy among them, so that I did not consume the people of Israel in my jealousy. Therefore say, 'Behold, I give to him my covenant of peace; and it shall be to him, and to his descendants after him, the covenant of a perpetual priesthood, because he was jealous for his God, and made atonement for the people of Israel.'"[8]

According to the Jewish historian Josephus, the liberation movement was started in A.D. 6 by Judah the Galilean, when he organized a revolt against direct Roman rule and taxation. The zealots probably received broad support from various sections of the community but, as is often the way with such things, they had a violent fringe movement attached to them called the Sicarii, who carried hidden daggers and used to assassinate Jewish collaborators, especially in the crowds at Festival times.[9]

We do not know whether Barabbas and Jesus had ever met, but we do know that Jesus was in touch with the movement he represented. Simon the Zealot was one of the twelve apostles, and it is possible that Judas Iscariot also belonged to their number. This introduces us to another approach to the problem posed by the evils and inequalities of human history. Pilate, as we have seen, did not think much could be done about it all, except to restrain and control it and "make sure the trains run on time". But there have always been a passionate few who have chosen not to run with the system but to run against it, to change it. They have a vision of a new earth where righteousness reigns, and they try to build it. If Pilate and his type are exponents of the politics of original sin, Barabbas and his friends are exponents of the politics of righteousness. They refuse to submit to the imperfections of human history and, in their different ways and different historical contexts, they identify the evil that has to be over-thrown if the kingdom of righteousness is to be ushered in. In the case of Barabbas, the identifiable evil was the Roman Empire: this was the source of the misery of the people of his country. The zealot of any time or place has a clearly identified target which is the cause of the misery he seeks to eradicate: he knows what pushed the first domino, and he is out to remove it and get the dominoes upright again. That first domino has been variously identified by the zealots of history as Capitalism or Socialism; too much Government or not enough Government; Religion or Atheism; Authority or not enough Authority; too much Freedom or too much Control. The objects of zealotry are kaleidoscopic in their variety, and there is usually considerable truth in their objectives, though in gaining them they usually overreach and set off a reaction

that starts to reverse the process. They are the essential com-
plement to the cynicism of managerial politicians, who are
contemptuously dismissed as pragmatists, while the zealots
take pride in their principles and convictions. But history
seems to teach that, although Barabbas may occasionally win
the revolution, it is always Pilate who ends up managing it.

We can be fairly certain that Jesus offered a measure of
validation to his zealot friends, though he refused to be drawn
into their plots. He knew what was in man, we are told,
knew that the misery of human nature was a more complicated reality than visionaries and revolutionaries realize, but
he did share their anguish at the ugliness and inequality of
human society. We do not know what he thought of the
release of Barabbas, but the irony of a machine politician
offering a sop to the local revolutionary cell in order to keep
things quiet would not have escaped him.

If Pilate tries to manage human structures, and Barabbas
tries to change them, the third approach to the mystery of
human sin is in many ways the most profound and effective
of all. This is the approach represented by religion and morality, the approach of those who were primarily responsible for
the death of Jesus, the Temple authorities in Jerusalem. They
believed that the root cause of human misery lay in the will
of the individual, and that that will had to be disciplined and
changed. A corrupt tree cannot bring forth good fruit, they
would have said. As long as human beings are unreformed
and corrupt, their institutions will be evil, but a good tree will
bring forth good fruit: a society of men and women who
have achieved personal righteousness will be a righteous
society. And this can be achieved only if men and women
stick to the rules of religion and morality, rules that have
served as instruments for the formation of character and
personality for centuries.

There is a certain kind of interpretation of the New Testament that paints the Pharisees, the great upholders of religion
and law, as a bunch of frauds and phonies, interested only in
the praise of others. Well, doubtless there were some like
that, but the religion they represented was one of the best
that human nature could achieve, and it did result in a moral
character that was heroic in its discipline and often wise in its

guidance of human nature. The tragedy was that even here the human disease penetrated and had its most devastating impact upon the highest expressions of human nature. The law, which was meant to be a means to the perfection of human nature, became an end in itself that increasingly stunted and confined human nature. It was because religion offered human nature the best chance, that its corruption could be so awful, and even at its best it did not work because it could not actually *change* human nature. Sometimes it modified it radically, kept it under control, tamed its wilder impulses, but often at the price of a more subtle form of spiritual sin which invaded the will and resulted in a harsh and unlovely self-righteousness that could be devastating in its censoriousness towards the weak. Human nature was so profoundly flawed that it could use anything, even the highest things, as a mode of its selfishness. That is why Jesus said that the conventionally sinful – the prostitutes and collaborators – went into the Kingdom of Heaven first: they were under no illusions about their weakness; while the morally pure could often be unaware of their pride and the extent to which they used their religion as a vehicle for their own egotism.

We know that while Jesus challenged the defenders of the law because they often put it above the needs of people, he did affirm the law, claiming that he wanted to fulfil it, not abolish it. But it is significant that it was the religious who were most inflamed against him. No emperor likes a poor man to tell him he has no clothes on, especially if he knows in his own heart that he is naked, and this was the kind of effect Jesus had on the religious. The best of them were not able to hear him, precisely because they had so much invested in their image of themselves. Judgement, however lovingly expressed, is hard for any of us to bear, and this man in his wounding simplicity judged people to the very ground of their personality, so that they either had to fall at his feet and admit their need or they had to remove him out of their sight. And that is still his effect when we really listen to him.

So Jesus to some extent affirmed and to some extent judged all the ways we try to deal with our own nature. He sympathized with Pilate, the managerial realist, but could not condone his absence of principle. He admired the ideals of

Barabbas and his sort, but judged them because of their lack of self-knowledge, their illusions about themselves and their motives. And he profoundly identified with the search of the religious for perfection, but faulted them for failing to recognize the profundity of human imperfectibility. We need our realists, idealists and perfectionists but even in combination they are unable to resolve the mystery of human nature. We are the disease we suffer from and we cannot be our own cure, or give ourselves absolution. Jesus sympathized with us, understood why we had to kill him, have to go on killing him: *"Father"*, he said, *"Father, forgive them, for they know not what they do."*[10]

VII

GOLGOTHA

Some years ago I was impressed by one of those very slick
television commercials we see nowadays. A young man
boards a train at St Pancras Station in London and gets into
one of the old compartments with three seats a side. He pulls
a thriller out of his coat pocket, a story about murder on the
Orient Express, and is soon engrossed in his book. Gradually
as the story takes him over he starts looking with suspicion
at his fellow passengers: the pretty girl opposite him begins
to look beautifully sinister and seductive, and when she opens
her handbag he fancies that he sees a gleaming stiletto; the
ineffective-looking vicar beside her, with the tobacco ash
cascading down his shirt front, on closer examination begins
to look like an evil and scheming prelate who plots the
overthrow of governments and the destruction of kingdoms;
and the stockbroker in the corner, wearing the tasteful tweed
suit, is almost certainly a master agent. The young man
realizes he is surrounded by enemies. He'd left London in a
normally grubby train compartment, thrown into the
company of a normally bored-looking set of passengers, but
by St Albans it had all changed. Everything had become
sinister. He looks round with fear and suspicion. Suddenly
the man in the corner smiles wickedly and reaches into his
pocket. "He's going for his gun", thinks the young man in
panic, and scrambles to his feet, throwing himself off the
train at some country station, far away from anywhere, but
safe. And as the train pulls away from the platform we see
the sinister looking gentleman who caused all the panic bring
from his pocket a packet of cigarettes, complete with Government health warning. A slick, well-made commercial, based
on a shrewd appraisal of human nature.

The young man in the commercial was the victim of what
we call projection, and the word is easy for us to understand.

We see it done every time we go to the cinema. The film in the machine behind us is projected onto the screen in front of us. That is a perfect image of a psychological phenomenon in which we project our own interior agenda from ourselves onto others. We have done it and we have seen others do it, often with tragic results. People who are angry and filled with turbulent feelings of unresolved hatred often project that inner turmoil onto others, accusing them of harshness or oppressive behaviour, interpreting the most insignificant remark as hostility. Sometimes it assumes a sexual form, in which a person may be filled with sexual anxieties or repressed and unadmitted desires, and these are somehow projected onto others, either in the form of obsessive suspicion about their conduct or of a loud and denunciatory puritanism. One of the best systems of self-examination is to discover the things we feel most strongly about and to ask ourselves why we feel that way. We will often find that projection of some sort is going on, at however low a level.

Projection is one of the things we do to distort reality and shape it into our own subconscious image, but there are others. We are flawed and complex creatures, and our wounds make us extremely sensitive to outside pressures. Anyone who has ever had a bad sunburn will remember how excruciating the weight of the lightest sheet feels upon a tender back, and anyone who has ever had gout will know how quickly normally comforting blankets can become deadly enemies as they press upon throbbing feet. As well as projecting our interior obsessions and anxieties onto others, therefore, we also react to others in a disproportionate way in those areas where we are most fragile. An insecure person will interpret even a kindly remark as a grave assault, if it is made flippantly, while an off-hand remark can bring on a major depression. Normal reality is distorted into strange shapes by our reactions to it, and our reactions are governed by factors that are sometimes beyond our control and to which we are often blind. This is why one of the most overworked phrases in the vocabulary of human conflict and misunderstanding is, "I didn't mean it". Often it is a lament for an argument that has got out of hand, but it is sometimes the puzzled response of an innocent person to a mysteriously upset friend who has suddenly gone into a passion or a sulk over a remark so inconsequential that he cannot even remember having made it. If we do this towards others whom we have seen and whom we know intimately, how can we avoid doing it towards that mystery we have not seen which we call God? We project our own shape and nature and all its conflicts onto that great blank screen in the sky, and back bounces a picture of God, twisted into our own shape, conformed to our own image.

One of the inescapable dilemmas of faith is created by this unavoidable tendency in us all to project our internal agenda onto external reality. Indeed, as we have already noticed in Chapter Two, one of the most potent refutations of belief in God is that it is a simple projection. This is not to claim that all religions unavoidably distort the nature of God to some extent, a claim most thoughtful people would accept, but that God himself is a pure creation of the human mind. The claim could be summarized in this way. We find ourselves apparently abandoned in a universe that is difficult to understand, and we have a strange need for purpose and meaning in our lives. Life brings to us many confusions and fears, including the fear of our own death and the knowledge that we have only one life to live. Yet we want our life to have ultimate meaning, we do not want death to be the end and we want guidance from somewhere about how we ought to live. Living in a permanent state of uncertainty about these matters of ultimate concern brings pain and anxiety, which threaten our lives with meaninglessness, so we create our own pattern and meaning to bring order and purpose to our lives. But what reason can we give ourselves for following a purpose devised by ourselves? The fickle and anarchic side of our nature needs to be controlled and ordered, but how can we ourselves take control over ourselves? What authority, what right can we discover that will compel our unruly natures to obey? We gain mastery by projecting our need for an authority that will control and direct our lives onto the delusion of an external and transcendent power to whom we owe obedience by virtue of our very existence. That power is the ground and cause of our being, and the end that awaits us. It clearly has authority over us and it can make sure its authority is vindicated, if only in the very long run. Fear becomes the antidote to lawlessness, just as divine purpose and guidance become the cure for the meaninglessness that haunts human life.

So the creation of the religious answer to life is a brilliant projection that does its work perfectly, controlling and con-soling in equal measure. Even after the ruse has been dis-covered there are many who argue that it must be retained in some form to save us from chaos and despair, though it has to be purged of its transcendent reference. We created it after all, though it often took a fearful revenge upon us, so we can retain what is good in it and abandon what is weak and dishonest. Henceforth we must be brave and honest enough to forge our own purpose and need for discipline and meaning, without having to scare ourselves into it by the placing of a great phantom Nobodaddy in the Heavens to keep us in order and console us in the face of death.

This account of religion attracts us by its very simplicity, and it clearly convinces some by its brilliantly straightforward solution to the problem presented by the mysteriously endur-ing survival of religion in a scientific culture that has system-atically refuted the explanations offered by religion for the existence of the physical universe. The projection theory is a brilliant hypothesis that is supported by our experience in other areas. We *are* capable of creating such a complex and subtle structure of belief for ourselves in response to our own needs and fears. It is not totally or universally persuasive, however, and it makes many people uneasy, not because it removes a comforting fantasy from them, but because it may be wrong. While it is almost certainly correct in many of the things it says about religious faith held for neurotic or unhealthy reasons, its explanations do not account for the existence of the saint or religious genius. The argument for the projection account of religion is based to a considerable extent on psychopathology. Projection of any sort seems to point to some level of self-absorption or narcissism in the subject. There is much of that at work among religious people, and for many of them faith is sometimes practised in a neurotic way. However, the religious type at its purest and highest does not seem to have these characteristics. The saint, the clear spirit, is characterized usually by innocence and purity of heart. Jesus told his hearers that it would be the pure in heart who would see God. In understanding that well-known but frequently misunderstood Beatitude, it will help us if we begin by emphasizing the last word, God.

Part of the problem for most of us in life is that we do not always see what is there in front of us. This is particularly true of our relations with other people: what we see in them is constantly modified or distorted by our own inner nature or "heart". We do not truly see *them*, because the picture we have of them is radically affected by our own complexities, projected from our own cluttered natures onto them. But there are always some people, purer in heart than the rest of us, who really see others as they are. These are people who have fewer twists or distortions in their nature. There is something clear about them, and when they look at us we really feel we are being seen as we are. This can often be uncomfortable but it can also be liberating, as we feel ourselves being understood and to a very great extent accepted as we really are. And it works the other way as well. Just as our own inner complexities distort reality into some kind of falsehood so that we are not really able to see what is there, so do they obscure and camouflage the picture we are presenting of ourselves. Often this is done self-consciously and we play a part, adopt a role, pretend to be what we are not. But often it is because our own level of self-understanding is so limited that we do not really know ourselves. When we are seriously deceived about ourselves we often fasten upon characteristics we lack, though we admire them greatly, and persuade ourselves that we possess them. Or it may be that vices we deplore but possess in abundance are denied by us or are transparently camouflaged, the way bald men often unintentionally draw attention to their baldness by the elaborate ways in which they try to hide it. And even where comparatively straightforward people are confronting each other there is great scope for misunderstanding. What we say and what other people hear us say are often wildly at variance. Anyone who uses words professionally understands this, and tries to heed Max Warren's plea for what he called "quadruple thinking", in which we think out what we want to say, then think how the other person will *understand* what we want to say, then re-think what we want to say, so that, when we say it, the other person will think what we are thinking.

One of the purposes of psychotherapy is to help us understand more of what is going on in our own interior self and to help us remove some of the obstacles to straightforward living, where that is possible; or to develop strategies for living with or going round the obstacles that may stubbornly remain in our hearts. There is a similar process at work in most spiritual traditions of any degree of sophistication. They help us in our search for self-understanding by prompting us to make acts of radical self-examination, so that we can come to know what is in our own hearts, and to submit to a process of purgation or re-ordering of our ideas and values, so that we can be exposed to reality, including the real nature of the mystery that encompasses us.

We ought to pause, therefore, before accepting the dismissal of religious faith as a mere projection, because of the persistent testimony of the pure in heart that they see *God*, and not just some version of themselves in their encounter with the mystery that besets them. Spiritual traditions of any seriousness help us to cut away false projections and untrue images. They call us to die to the self that seeks comfort in illusion. Indeed, the pure in heart, the souls that do not get in their own way when they are contemplating the mystery of life, usually infuriate those whose religion is an elaborate device for unconsciously avoiding a true encounter with reality. This was certainly the effect Jesus had upon his contemporaries. In him we see a trust in God that is so radical and absolute that it reverses and transvalues normal human standards, and this is the result, not of personal psychological complexity, but of purity, clarity of heart, a transparency that meant that what he saw and talked about was what was really there, whether it was in the hearts and minds of those who confronted him, or was the transcendent reality he communed with in the heart of the mystery of prayer. For those who try to follow him in some way, even if it is from a great way off – like Peter lurking back in the crowd that witnessed his passion – Jesus is the true interpreter of God, the one in whom divine reality is really made known, truly manifests itself.

For most of us the divine is an abstraction for much of the time, a category to be argued about, puzzled over, doubted, but rarely known with passionate and personal intimacy. For Jesus, God was the central relationship of his life, and it was a relationship so personal and consuming that it cancelled all other loyalties, including family loyalties, and over-ruled all other impulses and desires, including the absolutely basic instinct to cling to life. His apparently inordinate behaviour can only be accounted for if it is seen as the consequence of an intimate relationship, so intimate that it can only be described in the language of kinship, as of a son to a father. For us the Fatherhood of God is an attractive ideal, an aspiration that sometimes comforts our hearts or modifies our conduct, but is still largely an abstraction. For Jesus, God was not about Fatherhood, or even love; God was "my father". His relationship can best be described as "sonship", and that was the only really adequate way the early Church could find to describe his closeness to God. The most extraordinary thing about Jesus was that he always pointed away from himself to God. Even when he drew attention to himself by some claim to an authority that took precedence over existing religious tradition, it was always in the name of "my father", to whom he was obedient and whose authority he shared. This was what infuriated most of the leaders of the religious community in Jerusalem. It was said that the common people heard him gladly because he spoke "with authority", and that probably means that he spoke directly, experientially, without all the hesitations and circumlocutions that most men and women use when they are talking about God, in order to cover up their bafflement and ignorance. And this is still the most challenging thing about Jesus. Many people find much to admire in him, yet ignore the central purpose and passion of his life, which was the doing of his father's will. The main fact about Jesus was that he believed in God with an immediacy that can only be the consequence of absolute reality, what we call sanity; or absolute delusion, what we call insanity. If there is nothing in the mystery that surrounds us that corresponds to the one Jesus called Father, then we can only conclude that Jesus was insane.

I use the word "insane" advisedly, knowing that it was

used of Jesus by his hearers as reported in the New Testament, including his own family, who were convinced that "he was beside himself", and tried to drag him home. The word makes sense precisely because of the absolute level of commitment we see in Jesus, even into death. There was a rather flippant saying that went the rounds years ago that captures what is at stake here. It was said that the difference between a neurotic, an ordinarily uncomfortable and muddled human being, and a psychotic, a person who has completely lost hold of reality and is technically insane, is that a neurotic builds castles in the air and a psychotic tries to live in them. For the purposes of this discussion we could say that for "castles in the air" we should read "God". Obviously, most of us fantasize about many things, in a muddled and sometimes anxious way. We may agonize about whether God really exists. Ruthlessly exacting atheists would probably say that most people who claim to believe in God were neurotics rather than psychotics, tinkerers with reality rather than absolute deniers of it, because they never absolutely commit themselves to faith in God. They hedge their bets by saying they believe in God, but by living as though they didn't. The true believer, on the other hand, the one for whom God is a present, vivid and quite personal reality, must, if there is no God, be insane, completely out of touch with reality and trying to live in unreality. Indeed, even to ordinary half-believing Christians, people like Jesus appear to be so unlike themselves as to be insane. They have abandoned all caution and prudence to the wind, and live the absolutely committed life, without compromise or anxiety. And the paradox is that people who live like this, the people we call saints or holy ones, do not have the brooding complexity and pain that characterizes the insane, the tortured ones who have split off from reality. Nor do they possess the insecurities and anxieties, the greeds and longings of the neurotic majority who are trapped into conforming to the going standards of the time. On the contrary, the closer to God they become, the more committed they are to the service of that absolute whose existence is so trenchantly denied by some of the cleverest people alive, the more simple and joyful and straightforward they become. If it is only the pure in heart who see

God, the converse also seems to be true, that those who really see God become pure in heart, are characterized by a sort of limpidity that is in total contrast to the murky and cluttered lives of hesitant and complex half-believers or unbelievers. The insanity of total surrender to God seems to lead to the highest types of humanity, clear and straight in their own natures, and willing and laughter-filled in their service of others. The paradox of sanctity is the strongest contradiction of the claim that religion is an unhealthy projection; but there is power in the accusation, nevertheless, because there are so few saints and so many compromised Christians. The important thing, therefore, is not to win the argument but to seek to become holy, to be steadily more and more conformed to the nature of God. This is what Jesus meant when he said that we must be perfect as our heavenly father is perfect. And this perfection is not a chilly abstraction, a sort of emotional frigidity; it is, rather, a completed human nature, a wholeness and generosity of personality and character that results in a happiness and harmony of being. The Gospel of John tells us that Jesus said he had come to make our life more abundant, not less; to fill it with meaning and joy, not empty it.

And the heart of the message he preached and lived was the disclosure of the true nature of God. He called himself light, meaning that in his light we see into the truth about God and can now abandon our complicated fantasies about the divine nature, all those intricate projections of our own needs and fears. It is true, of course, that the projectionist is still at work in all of us, and can be seen throughout history in what theologians and other thinkers have made of Jesus. Liberal thinkers tend to see in him the confirmation of their own highest virtues, which are love and kindliness. In this way they seek permission for their own ethical uncertainty, seeing in Jesus the counterpart of human tolerance. Conservative thinkers find in him confirmation of their own commitment to hard, factual and obeyable truth, seeing in him the counterpart of the human need for ethical certainty. Radicals read into him their own determination to disturb every established authority, finding in him the counterpart of human moral discontent. Monastics exalt his humility; revolutionaries cite his anger at injustice; eschatologists emphasize his hope in the faithfulness of God. But in truth we have to recognize that Jesus did not theorize about any of these things, though all theorists about them can find some resonances for their own thoughts in his words and actions. As Austin Farrer put it, Jesus lived God, or, even better, God lived him, and in him we encounter God, not ideas about God. In Jesus the purity of God calls out to us to come away from our own complexities and see the truth of the divine nature.

What we already know of the invisible mystery of God has come to us in what we call revelation, glints of light upon that great darkness, twitchings aside of the veil that hides the mystery from our eyes. These revelations have mainly been conveyed through men and women who are uniquely sensitive to the mystery of God. We call them prophets or seers, mystics or enlightened ones. They are closer to the mystery than we are, but something of the divine nature comes through them to us. But what they see is always to some extent distorted by what they are, and to an even greater extent by what history has made of their visions and insights. So all religious traditions are a strange medley of divine truth and human error. We receive some light from God, but we project much of our inner tensions onto that light and it comes back to us distorted out of shape, confused and confusing. We perceive mercy in God, but we also perceive anger; we find love in God, but we also see an overpowering hatred. What is the true picture? Is God absolute love or is God absolute demand? We find in scripture descriptions of our own weaknesses that are full of gentle understanding and forgiveness, and we also find descriptions that threaten us with final rejection into everlasting night. Our own conflicted nature, struggling with self-hatred and the longing to be accepted, is projected onto God and bounces back contradictory images at us, so that we do not know which image to accept. We know we are sick, yet we are commanded to be sound. Our nature is weak, yet we are ordered to be strong. It is small wonder that the religious are often tormented people, whose anguish and uncertainty turn them into persecutors and destroyers, working out their own insecurities in hatred of the human race.

The crucifixion of Jesus is the perfect image of that conflict in human nature, turning upon the good man, the straightforward man in whom there was no self-hatred, and banishing him from the earth. The impact of Jesus upon ordinary men and women was complex, but there seem to have been two main elements in it. In the first place, he penetrated to the heart of the human personality and showed it up in its true light. In Jesus we see the sense of demand that is one aspect of our image of God, raised to an unbearable degree. He painted a picture of sanctified human nature that seems to be beyond the reach of even heroic human effort. How can we control our own unconscious human impulses of ordinary lust and anger, so that we will not even feel desire, or experience the temptation to hit out at those who oppose us? Yet he told us that to look lustfully at a woman was already adultery, and to call our brother a fool put us in danger of Hell. In our fear and insecurity, which protects itself with possessions and money in the bank, how can we find the absolute freedom that gives all away and in poverty follows the naked Christ? Yet he calls us to imitate the lilies of the field and the sparrows in the treetops in a life without care and anxiety. He showed us the gulf between ordinary respectability, or even fervent religious commitment, and the blazing holiness of a God who demands complete abandonment of all desire, ambition, comfort and security. He allowed us no shred of illusion about ourselves, no comfort in our own status as good people. His most biting words were reserved for those we would think of as good: those who went to church and tried to lead responsible lives; those who worked hard and gave much of what they earned to those in need; those who did not desert their families or collaborate with the enemy. His point was not that these things were unimportant or to be despised, but that they could trap us into complacence about our own condition, and fill us with self-righteousness. For him the supreme reality was the invisible God and commitment to that God as an absolute, an absolute beside which everything else shrivelled into insignificance. His accusation was that we did not know that God, yet we used Him against one another. We used God to support our prejudices, projecting them onto him and claiming his mandate for discriminating against those we hated: Samaritans, women of the streets, people we disapproved of. We used God to pronounce people unclean, damned or far from mercy. We used God as the vehicle for our own dishonest anger and hatred. In fact, we *had* made God in our own image, so that we could control others in his name.

The proof of that accusation lay in the crucifixion. All turned against Jesus and condemned him in the name of their God, whether it was political expedience, revolutionary mysticism or moralistic religion. The very frenzy of the act – the scourging, so that his back was cut to the bone with the sharpened lash; the bullying and horse-play, favourite tricks of cowards who are full of inward uncertainty; and the torturing death by impalement, the ancient remedy for those who want to purge themselves of self-hatred by finding a scapegoat that will take away their own sins – shows the accuracy of the charge Jesus raised against them. They killed him in the name of God, because he had shown them that they did not know what God was really like.

And this is the heart of the mystery: Jesus not only raised the demand of God to an absolute degree, showing how far we were from his absolute righteousness, he also showed by his actions and parables what the nature of God was like. The holy God he revealed was also unconditional love and everlasting mercy. The anger projected onto him by humanity was wiped away, and we saw the Father running to meet the prodigal, not turning away from him; we saw in Jesus the friend of sinners, consorting with criminals and prostitutes, not reviling them. All that was necessary from us was the wound of honesty, what Jesus called repentance, that stabbing realization that we were weak, lost in a far country, with all our innocence gone from us, yet needing to be home again, needing to be embraced and accepted, the tears wiped from our eyes, the pride gone, the posturing at an end, ourselves at last, honest before God: "God be merciful to me a sinner", we cry, and instantly the mercy meets us, raises us, washes our face, puts on us a new robe and calls for the musicians. And we see it all there in the cross.

And when they came to the place which is called The Skull, there they crucified him, and the criminals, one on the right and one on the left. And Jesus said, "Father, forgive them; for they know not what they do". And they cast lots to divide his garments. And the people stood by, watching; but the rulers scoffed at him, saying, "He saved others; let him save himself, if he is the Christ of God, his Chosen One!" The soldiers also mocked him, coming up and offering him vinegar, and saying, "If you are the King of the Jews, save yourself!" There was also an inscription over him, "This is the King of the Jews."

One of the criminals who were hanged railed at him, saying, "Are you not the Christ? Save yourself and us!" But the other rebuked him, saying, "Do you not fear God, since you are under the same sentence of condemnation? And we indeed justly; for we are receiving the due reward of our deeds; but this man has done nothing wrong." And he said, "Jesus, remember me when you come into your kingdom". And he said to him, "Truly, I say to you, today you will be with me in Paradise".

It was now about the sixth hour, and there was darkness over the whole land until the ninth hour, while the sun's light failed; and the curtain of the temple was torn in two. Then Jesus, crying with a loud voice, said, "Father, into thy hands I commit my spirit!" And having said this he breathed his last. Now when the centurion saw what had taken place, he praised God, and said, "Certainly this man was innocent!" And all the multitudes who assembled to see the sight, when they saw what had taken place, returned home beating their breasts. And all his acquaintances and the women who had followed him from Galilee stood at a distance and saw these things.[1]

The words of Jesus ceased at last: the great heartbroken accusations, the parables that broke open the compassion of God, the sins he forgave and the forgiveness he offered the world of humanity, all that ceased. The Word of God that had become words again in the mouth of Jesus, words that still trouble and console us as they mix absolute demand with absolute consolation, all the words the Word uttered ceased; and the Word became flesh again, and offered that flesh to the smiters and its cheek to those who tore out the hair. The crucifixion was the final parable, the story that never ends, because in it we see the way of God with us for ever, submitting to our anger and self-hatred, letting us spend it upon his body and breaking our hearts by loving us through and in it. *"The Lord turned and looked upon Peter"*, as he looks upon us. *"Father, forgive them, for they know not what they do."*

It changes nothing, yet everything is changed. We are still more than half-afraid of the demands of God, caught as we are in the complexity of our own nature, with its fears and lusts. But we know that it is all right now, that something has happened that has made a difference even though we are no different. There is no more we can do to him. We have proved that we cannot kill his love for us. He has borne all our sins, everything we can throw against him. They are still in us, yet he has taken them away, taken away their power, because he has shown us that they cannot separate us from God. God will not let them, he will allow sin no power over us, no power that will hide his love for us. There is a great silence round the cross: all the anger is spent, the revilings cease, the noise drifts away, and Christ lies there near to death and his whisper travels through history:

"Do you not yet understand? I love you; love you enough to die for you."

VIII

GALILEE

To live well is difficult. In order to live well, to live wisely, we must know ourselves as we truly are, and we must have some knowledge of the true end or goal of human life. In other words, we must combine two very volatile ingredients: realism about ourselves and aspiration towards goodness. The self that is struggling towards its true end must be a self that knows itself. The difficulty here is created by what Evelyn Underhill called "the psychic rubbish heap", that clutter of fears, insecurities, ignorances and illusions that fills our unconscious nature and modifies, when it does not actually control, the chosen direction of our life. We are not entirely free to choose the true end of our life because we are often the victim of forces we neither control nor understand. Our choices are not ours freely to follow, even when we know what they ought to be; but an even greater difficulty is ignorance of our true end, the goal to which we should aspire. Are we, in fact, going anywhere? Is there anything to aspire to or is it just a question of taking what pleasure we can from the journey between birth and death, since there is no goal to which we can aspire and with which we can make contact as we travel? To get the best in-flight entertainment package on the journey between Nonbeing and Unbeing is one model of existence, prevalent, as we have seen, not only among unbelievers but among half-believers and wistful ex-believers, as well as the variety of I-want-to-but-I-can't-quite-believers. The message and life of Jesus speak to all the elements in this complex agenda.

First and last and above all, he pointed to God as the beginning and the end, the source of our life and its final goal. And we must not sentimentalize his picture of God, because it contains terror as well as absolute consolation. The mystery that tantalizes and troubles us, plucking at our sleeve, troubling us with dreams, surprising us with longings as we look out of train windows or hear the sobbing tail end of songs on somebody else's transistor, is pure holiness, flaming goodness. It is difficult for muddled and morally complex creatures like us to arrive at a real understanding of holiness, but a human saint is probably the best and most accessible way into the mystery we can discover. We will find that our saint has a capacity for goodness that is wholly positive. In most of us the good life has a great deal of strain about it. We recognize in ourselves a capacity for love and goodness, but it is in constant tension with an equally powerful capacity for self-destruction and sheer muddled negativity. Our good acts are often achieved at the cost of grim effort, and sometimes the effort shows. There is usually something vulnerable and unsteady about our aspirations, and those who buckle themselves most sternly to the moral life often show a high level of emotional strain in their character. The effort can take its revenge in a kind of harshness of temperament from which frailer spirits shrink. This is why moralistic religion is unattractive and makes virtue unappealing. All the emotional energy goes into developing one side of the personality, one side of the moral life, and gentleness and largeness of heart are lost. Pascal captured the dilemma perfectly when he wrote:

> I do not admire the excess of a virtue like courage unless I see at the same time an excess of the opposite virtue, as in Epaminondas, who possessed extreme courage and extreme kindness. We show greatness not by being at one extreme, but by touching both at once and occupying all the space in between.[1]

Holiness touches all the extremes at once and occupies all the space in between. The true saint possesses a sort of effortless goodness that does not distort the personality in any single direction, and it robs evil of its power to trouble and complicate. We may indeed feel judged in the presence of a holy one, but the judgement is self-judgement and it never seems to come from the good person. Most of us know what it is like to be judged, found wanting and dismissed by the morally superior, but that is not the effect a saint has upon us. We get, instead, a level of self-acceptance from such a one that kindles aspiration and longing in us. This was certainly the effect that Charles Williams had on W. H. Auden:

> For the first time in my life [I] felt myself in the presence of personal sanctity. I had met many good people before who made me feel ashamed of my own shortcomings, but in the presence of this man – we never discussed anything but literary business – I did not feel ashamed, I felt transformed into a person who was incapable of doing or thinking anything base or unloving.[2]

It is also true, of course, that if evil has really mastered us, then to be in the presence of a saint can be painful and tormenting. If we have lost all contact with truth and goodness, the presence of the holy can fill us with a powerful hatred. The whole subject of possession by evil is a difficult and complex topic, but there is no doubt that part of the reputation of Jesus depended upon his effectiveness as an exorcist. He cast out evil, and his very presence was a torment to those possessed of evil spirits, however we interpret that phenomenon. A classic example is provided by Mark in his account of the encounter between Jesus and the demoniac who lived in a graveyard. Mark paints a frightening picture of the wretched man:

> . . . he had often been bound with fetters and chains, but the chains he wrenched apart, and the fetters he broke in pieces; and no one had the strength to subdue him. Night and day among the tombs and on the mounts he was always crying out, and bruising himself with stones.[3]

When he encountered Jesus he cried out: "*What have you to do with me, Jesus, Son of the Most High God? I adjure you by God, do not torment me.*" That kind of torment in the presence of holiness is not confined to the possessed, unless we include in that category all who have given themselves over to mean, cruel, evil and disloyal conduct. People possessed by that spirit often show a hatred for the holy and good that is probably bred of an angry self-hatred and interior self-condemnation. But in most of us the battle within our nature is still being fought, and holiness can exert an appeal over us, even if it is only in the form of an overwhelming sense of loss and failure, a sense of having missed something incredibly precious to us by a self-willed inattentiveness.

The holy person has a sort of passionate simplicity that smiles on the just and on the unjust and treats each with equal gentleness. We get from such a one no sense of strain or stress, not even a struggle for goodness. It is not just that they have at last found it possible not to sin, but that they have long since found it no longer possible to sin. We get from them a sense of apparently effortless beneficence. Such a person is emptied of deceit and selfishness, and has the magnetic clarity of an absolutely still and clear expanse of water. It is notoriously difficult to capture the essence of such a being in words, which is why really effective and convincing portraits of sheer goodness are rare in literature. Most fictional accounts of high sanctity are bland and vapid, as though the pure flame of holiness were incapable of being translated into any language other than itself. This is also why it is impossible to capture the essence of the mystery of God in words. The only language that seems to come anywhere near the fringes of the divine mystery is the language of what we might call "unsaying", the language of positive negation.

In Jesus we find the supreme example of holiness, purity of being. Paul writing to the Colossians describes him as ". . . *the image of the invisible God, the first-born of all creation . . . For in him all the fulness of God was pleased to dwell.*"[4] And we see all the complicating effects of holiness or divinity upon sinful creatures in the impact of Jesus upon those who heard him and watched his actions. He provoked hatred and guilt, as well as adoration and longing. He was known as one who went about doing good, and some of the most reliable evidence we have about him points to his work as a healer and tells of his tenderness towards outcast groups. Part of the fulness of his nature is revealed in the contradictions that surrounded his reputation. He lived a life of absolute detachment, having neither wife nor any home to call his own; yet he made use of what was offered him by others, accepting their services and invitations. We know that he wore an expensive robe at the time of his arrest, probably a gift from the women who ministered to him, and we know that he was at least an occasional guest at good dinner parties in Jerusalem, so that he earned among his detractors a reputation as a gluttonous man and wine-bibber. This seems to point to the wholly positive nature of his holiness. His self-denial and poverty would seem to have had no neurotic root. It was a positive thing in motive and intention, rooted in that freedom of spirit and purity of heart that allowed him to accept abundance and abasement with equal joy and detachment. He was able to affirm and celebrate the glories of creation in all their heartbreaking transience without building his life-purpose upon them. His parables repeatedly underlined the same message. He told the story of the man who built his house on sand and it fell in a great storm. He reminded us of the melancholy frequency with which men give all the energy of their lives over to the pursuit of riches, filling their barns with plenty, but are unable to prevent the abrupt summons of death. But self-denial and abandonment of worldly success were not preached for their own sake. They were the necessary consequence of seeking the true success, the real treasure, for which the wise fortune hunter would sell up all that he had in order to buy the field in which the treasure was hid.

And this is where it becomes difficult for many of us, as I have repeatedly tried to show. We know we suffer from a famine of spirit, a great longing for that unknown good we are born remembering but cannot rediscover. We are not entirely sure that it exists, and what will become of us if we sell all that we possess, buy that field, dig it up all over and find nothing? So we hesitate and equivocate. We do not actually buy the field, but we may build ourselves a place near it and get permission to walk on it and look at it and wonder about it. It affects the way we live and in some ways rather ruins things for us. We neither have the courage to abandon all for the sake of finding the pearl of great price Jesus told us about, nor do we have the appetite or conviction for a single-minded assault upon a world emptied of divinity.

And it is here that we must turn to the second element in the getting of wisdom. It is important to know the true end to which we move, but it is also important to know ourselves, to know the nature and complexity of the creature that is struggling with its own destiny. And this, too, was part of the summons of Jesus. He pointed to God but he also pointed into the human heart, and he called us to understand ourselves so that we could repent. The word "repentance" has an old gospel-hall ring to it, and we must not lose that sense of urgent challenge and summons, but there is a profundity and complexity of human self-knowledge behind the word. It really means a change or reformation of mind, a getting of things in correct order and right perspective, and this has to start with ourselves. We cannot really know God, see God, until our heart is purified and no longer distorts our view of reality. Profound self-knowledge is difficult, but not imposs-ible to attain, because, for a variety of reasons, most of us hide from painful facts and prefer comforting illusions.

When we are young we identify with people we admire, and since we admire them we tend to see ourselves as being like them. This is the phase of imitation, when we try on different roles in life. The easiest part of this process of role-modelling by imitation is the copying of physical charac-teristics and eccentricities. We learn how to tilt our head to one side, just like the one we admire, or to walk with that attractively rolling gait, or to smile with the same lop-sided charm. The field of imitation is as wide as life, of course, and in the same generation one boy can be learning how to replicate the pelvic gyrations of Elvis Presley while another boy is trying to pick up the characteristics of his favourite saint. If we are religious in our youth we may learn to admire St Paul, so we try to copy his passionate and single-minded commitment to Jesus – until it begins to get in the way of stronger interests. Maybe we have picked up a little bit about St John of the Cross from the sermons of that pious young curate we had, so we start out on the life of prayer, cultivating the vocabulary of contemplation and trying out the sort of far-away looks we fancy mystics ought to have – until bore-dom sets in and we move on to a different role, such as fervent missionary, jaded theologian, passionate servant of the poor or someone who has been through it all and now knows it is all vanity and there is nothing new under the sun.

Most of us reach the stage when we realize we are not remotely like the people we once admired and tried slavishly to imitate, but the passing of this illusion need not lead to cynicism. It may lead to a modest idealism. We know now we are not like our heroes, but we decide that we can still learn from them if we work at it. We know we are not born to play in the First Division, but maybe if we practise hard enough we can scrape a place in the Third. But that phase ends, too. One day we realize that we are not good enough to play in the League at any level. This is the stage when we can, for the first time, begin to be in touch with the person we really are; not terrific, heroic, holy, clever or even particularly good. We are, in fact, very ordinary and rather weak. This may be the point where we are tempted to despair, especially if we still retain in our conscious or unconscious minds a guilty echo of the great challenge of Jesus to be perfect, to be the fullest possible version of ourselves. But it is here that Jesus and the witness of the New Testament rescue us from despair, although they still summon us into ever deeper realism about ourselves.

If Jesus is the point of the New Testament, the one who came to show us the true nature of God and the inevitability of his magnetic power over us, then Peter is the counterpoint, the one who shows us how stubbornly difficult it is to respond to that challenge, even when it is made quite personally to us. And the paradox is that it is Peter's very failure that is our greatest hope. Without his muddled and powerful presence at the heart of the gospels most of us would find them hopeless and heart-breaking documents. It is Peter who, almost against his will, opens up to us the true generosity of the Gospel of Jesus Christ.

I once heard Bishop Michael Ramsey lecturing on the Resurrection narratives in the four gospels. On the occasion to which I refer he talked about the account in John 21 where Peter, after all his denials and desertions, is reinstated by Jesus.

Just as day was breaking, Jesus stood on the beach; yet the disciples did not know that it was Jesus. Jesus said to them, "Children, have you any fish?" They answered him, "No". He said to them, "Cast the net on the right side of the boat, and you will find some". So they cast it, and now they were not able to haul it in, for the quantity of fish. That disciple whom Jesus loved said to Peter, "It is the Lord!" When Simon Peter heard that it was the Lord, he put on his clothes, for he was stripped for work, and sprang into the sea. But the other disciples came in the boat, dragging the net full of fish, for they were not far from the land, but about a hundred yards off. When they got out on land, they saw a charcoal fire there, with fish lying on it, and bread.

Jesus said to them, "Come and have breakfast". Now none of the disciples dared ask him, "Who are you?" They knew it was the Lord.

When they had finished breakfast, Jesus said to Simon Peter, "Simon, son of John, do you love me more than these?" He said to him, "Yes, Lord; you know that I love you". He said to him, "Feed my lambs". A second time he said to him, "Simon, son of John, do you love me?" He said to him, "Yes, Lord; you know that I love you". He said to him, "Tend my sheep". He said to him the third time, "Simon, son of John, do you love me?" Peter was grieved because he said to him the third time, "Do you love me?" And he said to him, "Lord, you know everything; you know that I love you". Jesus said to him, "Feed my sheep. Truly, truly, I say unto you, when you were young, you girded yourself and walked where you would; but when you are old, you will stretch out your hands, and another will gird you and carry you where you do not wish to go." (This he said to show by what death he was to glorify God.) And after this he said to him, "Follow me". Peter turned and saw following them the disciple whom Jesus loved, who had lain close to his breast at the supper and had said, "Lord, who is it that is going to betray you?" When Peter saw him, he said to Jesus, "Lord, what about this man?" Jesus said to him, "If it is my will that he remain until I come, what is that to you? Follow me!"[5]

I did not take notes of Michael Ramsey's lecture, and I know it is still unpublished, but I remember vividly the central point he made about this passage. He said that there were two types of Christian sanctity, the Johannine and the Petrine, and we must all belong to one or the other. John stands for self-forgetfulness. He is so self-effacing that we hardly find out anything about him, even in the gospel that is attributed to him by tradition. He seems always to be there, right up to the end, when they took Jesus to the cross, but he is utterly self-forgetful. It probably never occurred to him to flee or to consider his own position during those terrible hours. He went on doing what he had always done. He did not think about himself or what all this might mean for him. He went quietly on, right up to the cross. Then there is Peter, who is also always there, but always talking, always pushing himself forward, always very much in evidence. If John stands for self-forgetfulness, Peter stands for the need for self-surrender. He had to learn to surrender his ego, to hand over his turbulent selfhood. These are the two models of Christian sanctity, self-forgetfulness or self-surrender. If we cannot forget the self, we have to learn to surrender it.

Most of us are like St Peter. The Johannine type is not unknown, of course, but it does seem to be quite rare. These are the ones who are already pure in heart. They are not cluttered up by their own spiritual and psychological agenda, so they really see God, not the projection of their own pre-suppositions. They have what William Blake called "single vision": they really see things the way they are, because they do not get in their own way, like most of us. If we do not possess it, this kind of purity of heart or forgetfulness of self seems impossible to cultivate. If we are constantly aware of ourselves, constantly getting in our own way, then practising self-forgetfulness will simply become another exercise in self-expression: "Behold me, notice me. Can't you see how self-forgetful I am becoming? I hardly seem to think about myself at all these days. Self-forgetfulness is so liberating, don't you think?" Alas, we are either already forgetful of the self or we must learn, like Peter, how to surrender it.

Peter was very far from self-forgetfulness. He seems to have had a very strong sense of himself and a significantly complicated inner nature. He seemed to behave impulsively, reacting rather than acting, as though certain external pressures prompted automatic responses from him. He seemed always to be in front of an audience, either his own private

audience that constantly monitored his performance, or
the real audience of the world, which was very important to
him and influenced him strongly, leading him to fear of
ridicule and promoting in him a fatal tendency, in spite
of his courage and impulsiveness, to fall in line, almost
unconsciously, with the prevailing view. Let us look at some
of the ways in which this complicated man got it wrong.

He constantly misunderstood Jesus because he did not really
hear him. Everything said by his master was filtered through
that powerful and complex ego, and by the time it had reached
Peter it was likely to be distorted out of recognition. He was
trying to follow Jesus, of course, but he was also clearly
figuring out his own role in the movement and the likely
effect of the success of Jesus on his own prospects, here or
hereafter. This complex inability to understand, because
he was unable to hear straight, erupted when he tried to get
Jesus to repudiate the necessity of his suffering and death.
It was absolutely consistent with the muddled inspiration
of the man that he earned his sternest rebuke from Jesus
immediately after he had acknowledged his unique spiritual
significance.

And Jesus went on with his disciples, to the village of
Caesarea Philippi; and on the way he asked his disciples,
"Who do men say that I am?" And they told him, "John
the Baptist; and others say Elijah; and others one of the
prophets". And he asked them, "But who do you say that
I am?" Peter answered him, "You are the Christ". And he
charged them to tell no one about him.

And he began to teach them that the Son of man must
suffer many things, and be rejected by the elders and
the chief priests and the scribes, and be killed, and after
three days rise again. And he said this plainly. And Peter
took him, and began to rebuke him. But turning and seeing his disciples, he rebuked Peter, and said, "Get behind me, Satan! For you are not on the side of God, but
of men".

And he called to him the multitude with his disciples,
and said to them, "If any man would come after me, let
him deny himself and take up his cross and follow me. For

whoever would save his life will lose it; and whoever loses his life for my sake and the Gospel's will save it. For what does it profit a man, to gain the whole world and forfeit his life?"[6]

Peter's mistake is still an inescapable dilemma for most of us. We are all strongly tempted, if we are at all interested in Jesus, to line him up on our side, use him as a vehicle for or projection of our own ideas. We are so busy filtering his words through our own private hearing system that his word gets distorted into our words and we fail to hear *him*. Peter misunderstood and misheard Jesus, and he constantly intruded himself into his work. He behaved inappropriately, talking when he should have kept silence and acting when he should have done nothing. At the scene of the transfiguration of Jesus it was Peter who prattled on in an embarrassing way to cover up his anxiety.

> And after six days Jesus took with him Peter and James and John, and led them up a high mountain apart by themselves; and he was transfigured before them, and his garments became glistening, intensely white, as no fuller on earth could bleach them. And there appeared to them Elijah with Moses; and they were talking to Jesus. And Peter said to Jesus, "Master, it is well that we are here; let us make three booths, one for you and one for Moses and one for Elijah." For he did not know what to say, for they were exceedingly afraid. And a cloud overshadowed them, and a voice came out of the cloud, "This is my beloved Son; listen to him". And suddenly looking around they no longer saw anyone with them but Jesus only.[7]

According to John's Gospel it was Peter who tried to make a fight of it, when Jesus was arrested in the Garden of Gethsemane, cutting off a man's ear in the process. He did not lack courage when he was whipped up to it, but it was not the steady courage of the naturally brave; it was the blustering courage of the boastfully insecure, proved conclusively by the complete collapse of Peter after the arrest, leading to panic, flight and vehement denial of the one he truly loved.

So Judas, procuring a band of soldiers and some officers from the chief priests and the Pharisees, went with lanterns and torches and weapons. Then Jesus, knowing all that was to befall him, came forward and said to them, "Whom do you seek?" They answered him, "Jesus of Nazareth". Jesus said to them, "I am he". Judas, who betrayed him, was standing with them. When he said to them, "I am he", they drew back and fell to the ground. Again he asked them, "Whom do you seek?" And they said, "Jesus of Nazareth". Jesus answered, "I told you that I am he; so, if you seek me, let these men go". This was to fulfil the word which he had spoken, "Of those whom thou gavest me I lost not one". Then Simon Peter, having a sword, drew it and struck the high priest's slave and cut off his right ear. The slave's name was Malchus. Jesus said to Peter, "Put your sword into its sheath; shall I not drink the cup which the Father has given me?"[8]

Yet this was the man upon whom Jesus built his community and to whom he committed the care of his lambs. Perhaps it was Peter's turbulent humanity and flawed normality that led Jesus to choose him. If the offer of forgiveness and restoration had come through an obvious saint and hero, few of us would be able to acept it. The awful courage and absolute commitment of Jesus already undermines us and places an intolerable strain upon us. His message sometimes seems to suggest that there is no room for people who are incapable of heroic virtue and denial of the world. But because of Peter we know that that cannot be the case; there has to be room somewhere for the rest of us. The most encouraging thing of all is that when Jesus came to reinstate Peter on that beach in Galilee he did not bring with him a list of Peter's failures, an indictment of offences committed. There was no word spoken of that, no mention of those terrible denials. Jesus built on what was already solid in Peter, his known love for him. He knew Peter loved him and he used that love. Three times he asked him if he loved him, and Peter must have heard his own threefold denial as he spoke his love. He had loved Jesus even as he was denying him, and that same love was even now blotting out the memory of those denials. This is one of the ways Jesus still works: he transforms us through our love, and our love grows from the knowledge that we are accepted and understood, even in our failures. Luther called certain verses in John's Gospel "the gospel within the gospel", because they summarized the whole matter:

> For God so loved the world that he gave his only Son, that whoever believes in him should not perish but have eternal life. For God sent the Son into the world, not to condemn the world, but that the world might be saved through him.[9]

But the encounter that captures the gospel most completely is the extraordinary story of the woman who was a sinner and came to Jesus during a fashionable dinner party at the house of a Pharisee:

> And behold, a woman of the city, who was a sinner, when she learned that he was at table in the Pharisee's house, brought an alabaster flask of ointment, and standing behind him at his feet, weeping, she began to wet his feet with her tears, and wiped them with the hair of her head, and kissed his feet, and anointed them with the ointment. Now when the Pharisee who had invited him saw it, he said to himself, "If this man were a prophet, he would have known who and what sort of woman this is who is touching him, for she is a sinner". And Jesus answering said to him, "Simon, I have something to say to you". And he answered, "What is it, Teacher?" "A certain creditor had two debtors; one owed five hundred denarii, and the other fifty. When they could not pay, he forgave them both. Now which of them will love him more?" Simon answered, "The one, I suppose, to whom he forgave more". And he said to him, "You have judged rightly". Then turning toward the woman he said to Simon, "Do you see this woman? I entered your house, you gave me no water for my feet, but she has wet my feet with her tears and wiped them with her hair. You gave me no kiss, but from the time I came in she has not ceased to kiss my feet. You did not anoint my head with oil, but she has anointed my feet with ointment. Therefore I tell you, her sins, which are many, are forgiven,

for she loved much; but he who is forgiven little, loves little."[10]

In this incident the meaning of the cross is spelled out in words. If we ever learn to love in a totally generous, unself-regarding way, it will be because we have been first loved and have learnt to accept that love and the forgiveness it brought. The cross shows that love, and on the sea-shore of Galilee Jesus spells it out for Peter in words.

> "Simon Peter, do you love me, in spite of that turbulent nature of yours that constantly trips you up and complicates our relationship? Do you love me, even though you often despair of ever changing, and frequently look back in anguish at all the mistakes you have made? Simon Peter, do you love me? Because if you do, and I know that you do, then the past does not matter; I am not interested in it. I am interested in *you* and I know that as you grow in the knowledge that you are loved and forgiven, you will learn at last to surrender that complex nature of yours, and your example will one day encourage all my other friends who will in turn, in their way, struggle to be my disciples."

But we must not make the mistake of falling into the trap of the happy ending, as the camera zooms away from the figures on the shore of the Sea of Galilee, while the orchestra resounds and the chorus hits the allelujahs. We know that it did not work out like that for Peter. Peter went on very much as before. He was wrong in the dispute that erupted in the young Christian community over whether Gentiles had to be circumcised before joining the Church, and he behaved in a cowardly way rather than face up to the angry traditionalists in Jerusalem. Paul kept a record:

> But when Cephas came to Antioch I opposed him to his face, because he stood condemned. For before certain men came from James, he ate with the Gentiles; but when they came he drew back and separated himself, fearing the circumcision party. And with him the rest of the Jews acted insincerely, so that even Barnabas was carried away by their

insincerity. But when I saw that they were not straightforward about the truth of the Gospel, I said to Cephas before them all, "If you, though a Jew, live like a Gentile and not like a Jew, how can you compel the Gentiles to live like Jews?"[11]

And he acted like a self-righteous and sadistic bully towards Ananias and Sapphira, an elderly couple who joined the early Church during its communist phase, but anxiously kept back some of their capital in case it did not work out. As a result of Peter's verbal assault Ananias died of a heart attack and he was followed by his wife hours later:

> But a man named Ananias with his wife Sapphira sold a piece of property, and with his wife's knowledge he kept back some of the proceeds, and brought only a part and laid it at the apostle's feet. But Peter said, "Ananias, why has Satan filled your heart to lie to the Holy Spirit and to keep back part of the proceeds of the land? While it remained unsold, did it not remain your own? And after it was sold, was it not at your disposal? How is it that you have contrived this deed in your heart? You have not lied to men but to God." When Ananias heard these words, he fell down and died. And great fear came upon all who heard of it. The young men rose and wrapped him up and carried him out and buried him.
>
> After an interval of about three hours his wife came in, not knowing what had happened. And Peter said to her, "Tell me whether you sold the land for so much". And she said, "Yes, for so much". But Peter said to her, "How is it that you have agreed together to tempt the Spirit of the Lord? Hark, the feet of those that have buried your husband are at the door, and they will carry you out." Immediately she fell down at his feet and died. When the young men came in they found her dead, and they carried her out and buried her beside her husband. And great fear came upon the whole church, and upon all who heard of these things.[12]

That encounter between Jesus and Peter on the sea-shore did not seem to result in a miraculous transformation that ended the struggle in his own nature. But we can be certain that he went on loving Jesus in his own way, knowing that he was first loved by Jesus. This knowledge would have preserved him from despair and defeat, though it probably continually prompted him to increasing self-knowledge. He would be exposed to constant criticism and challenge from other followers of Jesus, such as the irascible Saul of Tarsus, and beneath his blustering defensiveness he would accede to their criticisms and move on another fraction of an inch, knowing full well that growth in the spiritual life is measured in fractions, rarely in leagues. And all the time he would wrestle with the absolute challenge of Jesus, puzzled by it yet inescapably caught in it. According to legend Peter struggled in his relationship with Jesus to the end of his life, achieving in old age the self-surrender that had eluded him in his youth. In one legend, which is consistent with the vacillation that characterized his life, he escaped from Rome during the persecution of Nero in A.D. 64 and was trudging along the Appian Way when he met Jesus going back towards the city. "Quo vadis, Domine?" he asked. "Where are you going, Lord?" "Back to Rome to die for you, Peter", came the gentle reply. And we are told that Peter turned round and went back to his death. With characteristically extravagant humility he insisted, according to the legend, on being crucified head downwards, saying that he was unworthy to die in the way that Jesus had. After a lifetime of love and failure, Peter finally surrendered.

Centuries later another flaming soul would wrestle with the same paradox and capture it in hauntingly obscure language:

> Modern Lives of Jesus are too general in their scope. They aim at influencing, by giving a complete impression of the life of Jesus, a whole community. But the historical Jesus, as He is depicted in the gospels, influenced individuals by the individual word. They understood Him so far as it was necessary for them to understand, without forming any conception of His life as a whole, since this in its ultimate aims remained a mystery even for the disciples.
>
> Because it is thus preoccupied with the general, the universal modern theology is determined to find its world-

accepting ethic in the teaching of Jesus. Therein lies its weakness. The world affirms itself automatically; the modern spirit cannot but affirm it. But why on that account abolish the conflict between modern life, with the world-affirming spirit which inspires it as a whole, and the world-negating spirit of Jesus? Why spare the spirit of the individual man its appointed task of fighting its way through the world-negation of Jesus, of contending with Him at every step over the value of material and intellectual goods – a conflict in which it may never rest? For the general, for the institutions of society, the rule is: affirmation of the world, in conscious opposition to the view of Jesus, on the ground that the world has affirmed itself! This general affirmation of the world, however, if it is to be Christian, must in the individual spirit be Christianized and transfigured by the personal rejection of the world which is preached in the sayings of Jesus. It is only by means of the tension thus set up that religious energy can be communicated to our time. There was a danger that modern theology, for the sake of peace, would deny the world-negation in the sayings of Jesus, with which Protestantism was out of sympathy, and thus unstring the bow and make Protestantism a mere sociological instead of a religious force. There was perhaps also a danger of inward insincerity, in the fact that it refused to admit to itself and others that it maintained its affirmation of the world in opposition to the sayings of Jesus, simply because it could not do otherwise.

For that reason it is a good thing that the true historical Jesus should overthrow the modern Jesus, should rise up against the modern spirit and send upon earth, not peace, but a sword.[13]

Mysteriously, Jesus still gets hold of people the way he got hold of Peter and Paul and countless others down the ages. This laying hold of people throughout history is one of the things the Church means when it talks about the Resurrection of Jesus. That absolute surrender of himself to the abyss of God, that plunging into the cruel deep of death, was indeed an end and it was felt as such. They all forsook him and fled, but they fled from him only to meet him coming the other way, as is often the case with Jesus. Even death is not a category that can contain him. What supervened between the death and the flight from the place where they slew him, and the meetings in a garden at daybreak or an upper room at nightfall, on a sea-shore at dawn or in a country village at dusk, is not something that has been ever settled. According to the only witness we have, the New Testament, the tomb was found to be empty on the third day, and his body was never found, though there followed a series of encounters with his baffled followers. The historical situation is no longer really examinable by us, though it goes on being fought over, largely in the name of different theological traditions. Some find the robust physicality of the resurrection stories an intellectual embarrassment, while others rejoice in the stumbling block they place before modern consciousness. Some who say they cannot make sense of the empty tomb incline to a spiritualistic interpretation of the evidence of the New Testament, while others insist that the New Testament knows only a Jesus risen in the flesh.

And the ways people encounter Jesus today seem to bear some relationship to these approaches to the accounts provided by the gospels. Some encounter him with a level of subsequent certainty that is almost physical in its positive emphasis. Others know him as the beloved stranger, always turning the corner a pace or two ahead of them, seen suddenly in a crowd or heard mysteriously under the silence of an empty church. For yet others he lives on as a sort of haunting of the present by the past they can never reclaim. Many of those who have loved him, perhaps most, cannot forget him and do not want to, so they keep close to the tradition that contains his memory, being constantly surprised at the way he continues to elude his official keepers and appears suddenly in their midst. He is still the divine stranger who lays upon us impossible burdens and forgives us all our sins.

He comes to us as One unknown, without a name, as of old, by the lake-side, He came to those men who knew Him not. He speaks to us the same word: "Follow thou me!" and sets us to the tasks which He has to fulfil for our time. He commands. And to those who obey Him, whether they be wise or simple, He will reveal Himself in the toils, the conflicts, the sufferings which they shall pass through in His fellowship, and, as an ineffable mystery, they shall learn in their own experience Who He is.[14]

IX

CROSSFIRE

Christianity is sometimes said to be a straightforward thing, difficult to practise but easy enough to understand. That is usually said by people who reduce it to a simple code of conduct, such as "loving your neighbour as yourself". There are doubtless many for whom that is a satisfactory description of the thing. There are many straightforward people in the world, after all, and they are only following their own nature when they put things cleanly and without complication into an understandable formula. Such people have great strengths and they often have a talent for action and decisiveness, but they also suffer from a great weakness: they lack what the Spanish philosopher Miguel de Unamuno called "the tragic sense of life". In many ways Archbishop William Temple was the finest exemplification of the straightforward and uncomplicated man. In a masterly pen portrait, Adrian Hastings describes his sheer intellectual mastery of so many areas of thought, his genius for reconciliation and his calmness, cheerfulness and "sense of rock-like unhysterical conviction". But Hastings goes on:

> Had he no faults? They were the reverse side of both his qualities and his achievement. So genial, so unpompous, so peaceable, so successful a man could in the last analysis not quite cope with the demonic, or just the obstinately unreasonable. Must there not be some rational formula to resolve each difference? He lacked in his own harmonious life the experience of passion, grave conflict, sheer tragedy.[1]

Yet passion, grave conflict and sheer tragedy are permanent elements in human history, intrinsic to the human condition, and they are eloquently reflected in the Christian experience. In fact, Christianity is a religion of tormenting paradox

135

that reflects the human condition. We do have a need and longing for simplicity and goodness and straightforwardness. That longing is clearly reflected in a certain type of art and literature that charms us by its seductive half-truths. It produces in us a kind of nostalgia for a world without the serpent, which we persuade ourselves we once knew or knew about, till it was corrupted by the spirit of this present age. In that other, prelapsarian era, life was like an animated Norman Rockwell poster, in which everyone and everything was intrinsically good, firmly and uncomplicatedly rooted in a happy family life that knew little strife and was itself part of a wholesome social order. The thing that seduces us about this idealization of the past or of a possible future is that it is partly genuine; it does answer to something in us that longs for what R. S. Thomas calls "the glimpsed good place permanent".

We long for a place in which marriages are stable and happy; all children are wanted and secure; and divorce and abortion are not even imaginable possibilities. In that place sexual relations add romance and tenderness to life, but they have been purged of their passionate irrationality and ability to destroy. And there are no psychologically awkward groups there, people with unusual and unpredictable needs who break up the perfect balance of community by fixing their sexual and emotional longings on hopelessly inappropriate objects. In that place there is neither hideous poverty nor ugly and ostentatious wealth. There are many differences between people, of course, but these differences are both fluid and organic. The inequalities that exist serve only to stimulate effort and aspiration, and never breed resentment. Our Eden, in fact, is without the three explosive elements that are the great enemies of private happiness and social harmony: lust, greed and envy.

We have all caught glimpses of that place of shining faces and pure, uncomplicated hearts, and we often discover in ourselves a hunger for an innocence that will permanently lift us out of the moral and psychological tangles that enmesh us, and the very intensity of the longing distorts our perceptions. We do remember Eden, but we have edited and expurgated our memories. We have forgotten the long boredoms that led us so often to the forbidden places. We have forgotten the tormenting discontents of lust, greed and envy. We have forgotten the intolerance we often felt for those to whom we were related and whom we genuinely loved. Above all, we no longer detect the simmering discontents and insecurities behind the happy and uncomplicated faces on the Rockwell tapestry. We are and always have been creatures in conflict with ourselves and with one another – not all the time, of course, and not with everyone, but enough to make the idealized portrait of human society more an expression of a longing than a representation of hard, actual reality.

And the paradoxes of Christianity uncannily mirror the dualities and ambivalences of human life. Jesus calls us to heroic innocence and self-sacrifice, to purity of heart and absolute love, and something within us answers the call, acknowledges its appropriateness and inevitability: "This would restore lost Eden, this *is* the way out and back, it is the obvious and essential precondition of the establishment of the glimpsed good place permanent, which some call the kingdom of heaven." Yet that call to holiness to which we respond with recognition and remembrance, as might an amnesiac woman to a face and voice from her most intimate past, is quickly joined by other voices and other memories that also come out of the accumulated history of our nature. The call of Jesus brings a sword, not peace of mind, because it sets up within us the disturbance of an unrealizable aspiration. And this tension is not felt only at moments of failure or only in the moral struggle. It is felt in prayer and at worship and during the very thinking we do about God. We are always on a threshold we never seem able to cross. We have a mysterious sense of the accessible presence of a mystery we cannot quite reach, and we strain from the threshold towards it. It draws us by its insistent elusiveness towards a fulfilment that awaits us, if only we could take leave of ourselves, somehow unbuckle ourselves from the harness that restrains us. But we are tethered in all sorts of ways, and the moral struggle is only the most obvious. We find it difficult to obey the law we have assented to with our hearts and minds, but even when we do obey, our obedience is somehow loaded, so that our very virtues seem to conspire against us. We are like winged creatures tethered to a rock, caught up to God by his beauty and torn away from him by our own weight. Or we could put it more positively and say that in spite of our exile we have one foot in Eden still, as Edwin Muir reminded us:

One foot in Eden still, I stand
And look across the other land.
The world's great day is growing late,
Yet strange these fields that we have planted
So long with crops of love and hate.
Time's handiworks by time are haunted,
And nothing now can separate
The corn and tares compactly grown.
The armorial weed in stillness bound
About the stalk; these are our own.
Evil and good stand thick around
In the fields of charity and sin
Where we shall lead our harvest in.[2]

These *are* our own and own them we must, the corn and the tares, the good desires and longings as well as the sheer heaviness in our nature that makes goodness such a labour.

But we are saved from despair and failure, or from the wrong sort of success, by the other element in the paradoxical appeal of Christ. He not only calls us to an impossible holiness; he offers us unconditional forgiveness. By his call to holiness he offers us not peace but a sword, the sword of endless moral and spiritual struggle, captured in Unamuno's famous epigram: "May God deny you peace but give you glory". But this has to be held in tension with the offer of a forgiveness so absolute that it can easily be mistaken for permission to abandon the moral struggle altogether. The offer of forgiveness without limit and without exception to those who own their need of it makes the essence of Christianity grace, not law; gift, not demand; good news, not condemnation. So the attempt to live out a particular and actual Christian life is like the string that is slung between the ends of a bow: it is the opposites, the contradictions that give it tension and power. In the case of Christian faith the tension is derived from the philosophically incurable paradox of the message of Jesus, who calls us to holiness and denial of the world, yet forgives us all our sins; who places impossible demands upon us, yet offers us full acceptance. Those who try to follow in this way know the meaning of the contradiction in their own lives. Though they can never offer a satisfactory resolution of it in words, they perceive its psychological efficacy. They know that the essential basis of any mature living is full acceptance, absolute assurance of worth and affection. When that is truly experienced and truly believed it creates the only possible context for joyful self-surrender. We love because we know he loved us first. Only the loved can love, and only absolute, unconditional love can convince us that we are, in fact, loved beyond all abandonment.

Paradox is a difficult thing to live with, especially when it creates a tension as extreme as this one, so it is not surprising that attempts are always being made to unstring the bow, resolve the contradictions in Christianity and make it something straightforward and practicable, instead of something curved and awkward to handle. The danger here is not in the way people do, in fact, select one end of the Christian paradox and emphasize it almost to the exclusion of the other, but that they do not admit what they are doing. Inconsistency of one sort or another is intrinsic to the human attempt to follow the way of Christ. The danger lies in unacknowledged and unexamined inconsistency. We are locked into history; we are imprisoned in our culture and yet we are at the same time captured by Christ and drawn towards his holiness. We could say that when we encounter the purity and absoluteness of Jesus we are permanently wounded by it. If there is no wound there has been no encounter. Being wounded, being made vulnerable, partaking somehow in the sufferings of Christ, is at the heart of our encounter with Christ and helps us interpret the meaning of the cross. In Christ we encounter demand and forgiveness, and the cross is both the emblem of that encounter and its abiding method. We assent to the call to holiness and yet constantly acknowledge our failure and need of forgiveness. We are haunted by transcendence, though we live in a world purged of wonder. We are in permanent conflict with ourselves, caught between belief and unbelief, moral struggle and moral weariness, and we are wounded by the conflict. Disoriented by the crossfire, it is not surprising that we dash for cover.

Ordinary believers often try to resolve the conflict practically by winding themselves up to a sort of perfectionist enthusiasm, on the one hand, or by removing the uncomfortable element of demand, on the other. They either move the target so far away that only a few exceptional archers get near it, or they move it round at will to catch the arrows where they fall, so that everything qualifies and everyone gets a prize. So Christianity becomes ruthlessly absolutist, as we whip ourselves up to believe the truth and obey the rules; or it becomes weakly accommodationist, as we supply ourselves with justifications for doing or believing anything we want to. We either emphasize the demands of Christ and exclude his grace and forgiveness, or we emphasize his grace and forgiveness and ignore his demands.

Theologians, professional religious thinkers, often try to resolve the conflict theoretically by a comprehensive explanation that turns Christ into an abstraction, a theological or philosophical problem with an intellectual solution, rather than a personal encounter that has to be endured and lived through like any other relationship. This is the point of Albert Schweitzer's great challenge to professional theology in *The Quest for the Historical Jesus*, from which we have already quoted. He tells us there that modern theology is too general in its scope, because it aims at giving a complete or universal explanation of Jesus. Theologians operate in the great community of ideas, they are part of the great intellectual conversation that characterizes human civilization. According to Schweitzer, Jesus does not encounter people in that way. He writes:

> The historical Jesus . . . influenced individuals by the individual word. They understood Him so far as it was necessary for them to understand, without forming any conception of His life as a whole, since this in its ultimate aims remained a mystery even for the disciples.[3]

Indeed, Schweitzer himself is the best possible justification of his own claim. His great book did not resolve the enigma of the historical Jesus because it, too, tried to give a complete explanation of his life, tried to supply a historical key that would account for it. Schweitzer the theologian interpreted Jesus as a passionate eschatologist who flung himself onto the cross in order to force God to intervene directly in the human tragedy. But Schweitzer's "historical Jesus" was just as unsatisfactory an explanation of Jesus as the ones it replaced or the ones that have followed it. The point is not to explain Jesus but to encounter him. Schweitzer the theologian seemed to leave Jesus hanging in despair on the cross of his own explanation, but the whole world knows that that was only in his book. Some other version of Jesus met Schweitzer the man by the lake-side and spoke the words: "Follow thou me!" After years at Lambarene in his jungle hospital we can apply to Schweitzer his own words at the end of his book:

> And to those who obey Him, whether they be wise or simple, He will reveal Himself in the toils, the conflicts, the sufferings which they shall pass through in His fellowship, and, as an ineffable mystery, they shall learn in their experience Who He Is.[4]

Nevertheless, the human beings who encounter Jesus and respond to him do so from within particular histories that are also part of universal history. No one encounters Jesus in a historical or cultural vacuum. We come to him from within our own experience and we bring that experience into our subsequent relationship with him. Indeed, as we have already seen, it is that encounter between men and women who are inextricably bound to human culture and one who transcends the ambiguities and inconsistencies of the historical order that sets up the very conflict that characterizes Christian history. As men and women wrestle with the meaning of Christ in their experience of him, they inevitably try to understand and explain his impact upon themselves and upon history. These explanations and attempts to understand or synthesize human experiences of Christ are as unsatisfactory as they are inevitable. The history of Christianity is the history of the clash of those attempts at understanding and explanation. And it is this turbulence that makes Christianity such an uncomfortable

religion. In Richard Niebuhr's masterly book on this permanent conflict within Christianity, *Christ and Culture*,[5] he
examines how men and women have actually responded
to the tension that is built into Christian history by the
unforgettable summons of Christ, on the one hand, and the
ineluctable grip of human culture, on the other. He tells us
that there is no escape from that dilemma, nor any permanent
resolution of it.

> . . . an infinite dialogue must develop in the Christian con-
> science and the Christian community. In his single-minded
> direction toward God, Christ leads men away from the
> temporality and pluralism of culture. In its concern for the
> conservation of the many values of the past, culture rejects
> the Christ who bids men rely on grace. Yet the Son of God
> is himself child of a religious culture, and sends his disciples
> to tend his lambs and sheep, who cannot be guarded without
> cultural work. The dialogue proceeds with denials and
> affirmations, reconstructions, compromises, and new de-
> nials. Neither individual nor church can come to a
> stopping-place in the endless search for an answer which
> will not provoke a new rejoinder.
>
> Yet it is possible to discern some order in this multiplicity,
> to stop the dialogue, as it were, at certain points; and to
> define typical partial answers that recur so often in different
> eras and societies that they seem to be less the product of
> historical conditioning than of the nature of the problem
> itself and the meanings of its terms.[6]

This reminds us of Schweitzer's way of setting out the problem:

> The world affirms itself automatically; the modern spirit
> cannot but affirm it. But why on that account abolish the
> conflict between modern life, with the world-affirming
> spirit which inspires it as a whole, and the world-negating
> spirit of Jesus? Why spare the spirit of the individual man
> its appointed task of fighting its way through the world-
> negation of Jesus, of contending with Him at every step
> over the value of material and intellectual goods – a conflict
> in which it may never rest?[7]

In that conflict two great opposing points of view emerge in history which create a continuum along which most Christians are placed. These extreme responses set the boundaries, but there are a variety of mediating types in between who seek some sort of synthesis between the two great opposing views. These responses have been called by many names in theological and cultural history. In this book we have used the terms "fundamentalism" and "accommodationism", though we might just as usefully describe them as "radicalism" and "liberalism". Niebuhr in his typology calls them the "Christ against Culture" type and the "Christ of Culture" type.

Fundamentalists at all times stress the distinctiveness and discontinuity between religion and society. God and his will always stand over and against human history in judgement. And that judgement is always mediated through a revelation that is simply given to human beings with or without their consent. It stands there as authoritative, whether they hear and acknowledge it to the letter, or put their reason to work on it in an effort to understand it, arrive at some willed consent to it. The fundamentalist or radical Christian heightens revelation at the expense of reason. Though reason may be used to justify and explain revelation, it can never overturn it, because it is the given thing, the thing from beyond that bears within itself its own authority over and against our ability to apprehend it. We are called to submit, not to interrogate it. We see this theme of absolute submission played out in many ways in Christian history, from the Protestant fundamentalist who seeks to govern her life by total obedience to the letter of scripture, to the Roman Catholic ultramontanist who heightens the authority of the Pope to an absolute degree. Sometimes absolutists of this type go out of their way in search of commands that are at the extreme of contradiction to reason. They almost lust after absolute demands and impossible beliefs that set them at variance with the muddle and imprecision of an equivocating world. For them God, or the divine institution that mediates the will of God, is the one great objective fact of life, and men and women are called to acknowledge the divine reality and be obedient to the divine will.

This means that it is the task of theology to point to and

explain the significance of the contents of the revelation of God that has been deposited in history like a great archaeological site. Theology does not have a creative or exploratory role; its task is to label the contents of revelation and explain them to human beings, because their happiness and salvation depend upon exact conformity to the will of God as made known in the deposited revelation.

If the theologian's role is that of cataloguing and explaining the account given of the divine nature in the revelation, it becomes the task of the Christian moralist to codify and enforce the laws of God given in the same revelation. Fundamental or radical Christians usually end up as legalists who make sanctification the prerequisite of grace, not its consequence; the condition on which forgiveness is offered, rather than the joyous response to forgiveness already received. Jesus becomes the great lawgiver whose commandments are in accordance with right reason. Human corruption is located not in human nature, but in human culture, in the structures and institutions that have evolved in human history. Fundamentalists have little understanding of the extent and depth to which culture enters our very nature and modifies and forms it, so they tend to become crusaders against society in its contemporary manifestations, urging Christians to battle against its current imperfections and separate themselves from it. A clear line of separation is drawn between the children of God and the children of the world, and God's children are called to go out from their midst and be separate in their ways if not in their actual habitations.

The main paradox of moralistic Christianity is that it often ends by denying the revolutionary grace of God's unconditional love as preached by Christ; and by emphasizing one aspect of his message to the exclusion of the other it excludes the very people Christ came to seek and to save, the unrighteous, the sinful, the unrespectable, the ones who were "in need of a physician". The result is the embourgeoisement of believers, who tend to become model citizens and business people, accumulating the substance and power of the very world they set out to deny, while the losers and rejects of the world, whose weaknesses prevent them from being conformed to the world, are made to feel rejected by the Church as well.

The result is the kind of religion that provoked the wrath of the Russian Nobleman in Rebecca West's novel *The Birds Fall Down*:

> . . . the piety of the English is a mockery. They want a prescription for social order, and union with God means nothing to them. So they pretend that this is what religion is for: to teach men and women to be moral. But we Russians know that religion is for the moral and the immoral. It is the love of God for man meeting with the love of man for God, and God loves the vicious and the criminal and the idle as well as He loves the industrious and the honest and the truthful and the abstinent. He humbles himself to ask for the love of the murderer, the drunkard, the liar, the beggar, the thief. Only God can achieve this sublime and insane relationship.[8]

Niebuhr describes the fundamentalist or radical position as "necessary and inadequate". He points out that the single-heartedness and sincerity of the great representatives of this type are among their most attractive qualities:

> They have not taken easy ways in professing their allegiance to Christ. They have endured physical and mental sufferings in the willingness to abandon homes, property, and the protection of government for the sake of his cause.[9]

Their protests against the intrinsic corruptions of organized society "have maintained the distinction between Christ and Caesar, between revelation and reason, between God's will and man's".[10] And one of the interesting paradoxes at work here is that radical Christians often accomplish what they do not necessarily set out to achieve – social reform. They have gone out from the midst of the world, seeing it as contrary to God and beyond redemption, yet their very rejection of it plays an important part in its purification. Medieval monasticism became one of the great preservers and transmitters of culture, and it had a profound impact on the politics and economic development of Europe and America. Protestant sectarians, by their defiant refusal to conform to the established religions of their day, created a process which ended in guaranteeing religious liberty to all members of society. And Quakers and Tolstoyans "intending only to abolish all methods of coercion, have helped to reform prisons, to limit armaments, and to establish international organizations for the maintenance of peace through coercion".[11]

Though this position is inadequate, therefore, it constantly needs to be given, if only because without it other Christians lose their balance. Christians need constantly to be challenged by the absolute authority of Christ to reject the world and its inevitable tendency to relativize all value, to compromise with evil and to flee from sorrow in the face of death into a desperate absorption in the pleasures of life.

Important as it is, however, it is not enough and it never achieves in action what it affirms in words, which is the possibility of sole dependence on Jesus Christ to the exclusion of the world and its influence. We cannot divest ourselves of our culture – it is in us, and radical Christians are always making use of the very society which they reject so dramatically. Early radical Christians borrowed what they needed for their common life, but had not received from their own source of authority, from the laws and customs of those from whom they had separated. Jesus Christ is, in fact, very unsatisfactory for legalists to deal with, because there are so many areas of responsibility he leaves to the private conscience. On the one hand, he seems to play into their hands by the absoluteness of his demands, but he fails them by refusing to paint in the details that are so necessary for the codification of any system that is likely to work. He painted in large aspirations, great ends to be sought after, but he failed absolutely to take care of the minute detail required in developing legal tactics for the achieving of those ends. For the law to work absolutely it has to be drafted in such a way that it closes as many loopholes as possible. Later legalists in Christian history have had to spend a lot of time filling in the detail that Christ left uncoloured. Jesus seems to have been swift in sketching dramatic aspirations in general terms, but significantly evasive when it came down to judging particular cases: "Man, who made me a judge and divider over you?"; "He that is without sin among you let him cast the first stone"; "Render unto Caesar the things that are Caesar's and unto God the things that are God's". His disciples have been bolder and have filled in the gaps he left, but they have had to raid other traditions, other cultures, and in the case of fundamentalists who reject worldly society outright, they come perilously close to the great anti-Christian heresy of Manichee, who divided the world into a material realm governed by a principle opposed to Christ, and a spiritual realm guided by God. Most groups of this sort end up by claiming to be in sole possession of the Spirit of Christ whose private directives they quote endlessly; but they purchase their certainties by separating God from his world and its normal processes. They create a universe that is a metaphysical minefield, governed by an enemy, sown with explosives, in which only those get through to safety who have hit upon the inner secret, the private knowledge, the map known solely to the initiates. This picture of a divine sadist who makes life as hard as he can for his children is completely different from the New Testament picture of a God who loved the world so much that he sent his only begotten son into it, not to condemn it but to bring it more abundant life.

But the main thing to note about groups who give this answer is that they do not themselves succeed in living by it. The difference between radical groups and other Christian groups is often only that the radicals fail to recognize what they are doing, and continue to speak as though they were actually different from the world. According to Niebuhr, the radical Christian has not solved the problem of Christ and Culture, he only seeks the solution along a certain line. He borrows endlessly from the culture from which he claims to be separated or which he passionately repudiates. Modern American versions of this ancient tendency are particularly good at borrowing communications and money management technology for their own use, but they also absorb and assume the timeless validity of a whole range of attitudes and values which are transmitted through the agencies of this fallen world. Whether they acknowledge it or not, they are organically connected to the world they seek to repudiate, they are bound to it by tissue and subconscious formation. If they want to follow Jesus they must learn to follow him in some sense from within the world, because they cannot ever follow him outside it.

The other main response to the conflict created by the demands of Christ and the insistent pressures of human culture is what I have called accommodationism. Niebuhr describes this as "the Christ of Culture" position. There are always those who feel no great tension between the Church and the world. They interpret culture by Christ and see Christ largely through culture. Christ and culture become harmonized. In this view, Christ is the great educator or reformer, the great liberal progressive, who unfolds the future for us. Accommodationists are "once-born" types, to use William James' famous classification. They are healthy-minded, unshadowed by the tragedy and complexity of human history. The modern version of this type is the Christian liberal, but they go back to the earliest days of Christianity, as do their opposite numbers in the fundamentalist camp.

According to Niebuhr, the Judaizers were the earliest accommodationists. For them Jesus was not only the promised messiah but the messiah of the promise, as this was understood by them. There was to be no social or cultural dislocation for the people of the old covenant. Jesus the Jew called people to him from within Judaism and kept them there. No emigration was necessary, no major disruption of ancient practice was required. It is worth remembering that the Judaizers nearly had their way in the early Church, intimidating Peter into episodic conformity with their attitude. It was Paul, that complex fundamentalist, who fought the Judaizers and succeeded in separating the Christian movement from an embrace that would have suffocated it at birth.

The most extreme example of the accommodationist attitude, which interprets Christ wholly in cultural terms and tries to eliminate all tension between Christianity and the world in which it is set, was represented in the Hellenistic world by various groups called gnostics. Gnosticism, from the Greek word for knowledge, was an attempt to reconcile Jesus with the science and philosophy of the time. Gnostics sought to raise Christianity from the level of belief to that of intelligent knowledge and so to increase its attractiveness and power. Their method entailed the naturalization of Christ within the current attitudes of intellectual society. Gnostics, ancient and modern, always find their greatest success in helping men and women adjust to this difficult and indifferent world. They accomplish this by easing the tensions between faith and life. They are good at helping people live with and through the world, not against it, by learning to accept themselves, rather than in seeking change or transformation.

This gnosticizing dynamic is a permanent element in theological history. On the one hand, the accommodationist seeks to make Jesus congenial to the cultured despisers of religion by creating contemporary interpretations of him, and though the interpretations vary enormously they all reflect the spirit of the age and place in which they are minted; and on the other hand, the accommodationist, usually for entirely pastoral and compassionate reasons, tries to make people comfortable with themselves and their situation by legitimating their compromises and cowardices.

Niebuhr, in his balanced way, seeks to affirm as much as he can in what he calls "cultural faith". He notes that it is inevitable and at the same time a profound sign of Christ's influence in history. He points out that most of its critics share some of the attitudes they set out to reject. For instance, Fundamentalist Christians usually reject what they perceive as the false acculturation of Liberal Christians, but they usually offer their criticism from another type of cultural loyalty. They may show this, for example, by their passionate desire to preserve the cosmological and biological notions of older cultures, notions which have nothing to do with the Lordship of Christ. Dean Inge's famous epigram is often quoted by critics of cultural faith: "*He who marries the spirit of the age will one day find himself a widower*"; but the quotation only serves to underline the point. Critics of liberal Christianity attack it for its slavish dependence on the *Zeitgeist*, but they inevitably criticize it from the point of view of another type of captivity to time. They usually criticize the compromises of today from the vantage point of the compromises of yesterday, but that is no gain. Inge was right, but not in the way he meant. We are, in fact, all widowed in one sense, because we are ineluctably bound to our time, with all its partialities and limitations, because it is the only time we are given.

But there are more positive ways of defending accommodationism. By it Christ is identified with what some people conceive to be their finest ideals, their noblest institutions and their best philosophy. Though they may aim at the reform of culture rather than the extension of Christ's Kingdom, they contribute to the latter by helping men and women understand something of the Gospel. So cultural Christians, liberals, accommodationists, call them what we will, are to some extent missionaries to intellectuals. Christ was himself a wise man, and this struggle for intellectual integrity among some of his followers points to that continuity. It is this impulse that has helped to keep Christianity from being a withdrawn sect.

Nevertheless, it is important to recognize that this position is as partial and inadequate as its opposite. It is impossible to remove the offence of Christ or make him palatable to the world's taste, so the cultural Christian has to doctor Christ to make him acceptable. The New Testament has to be re-written or interpreted in a way that makes it conform to current attitudes.

But Jesus Christ never seems to suffer himself to be held hostage by any group or movement for long. He always seems to rise from within the very groups that imprison him to challenge their assumptions. The gravest charge against accommodationists or cultural Christians is that their loyalty to contemporary values outweighs their loyalty to Christ, so that his name becomes an incidental brand or label on attitudes that are held, in fact, with no reference to him. Whether it is conformity to contemporary racial values, as among German Christians under the Nazis or South African Christians under the Nationalists; or conformity to contemporary sexual values, as among Christians in America and Europe today, the dynamic is the same: the prevailing norms of society are anointed by the high priests of cultural accommodation, in all sincerity, as in conformity with the mind of Christ. Fundamentalists allow no development in their understanding of the relationship between revelation and history, so they cut themselves off from Christ's impact on history. Accommodationists do the reverse: they allow the values disclosed in revelation no role in judging developments in history, so they cut themselves off from Christ's abiding presence in revelation.

Fundamentalists and accommodationists are uncannily balanced against each other with an almost reverse precision in two other ways. We have seen that fundamentalists exalt revelation against reason, authority against free consent. Accommodationists do the reverse. Unlike the fundamentalists they are aware of the ways in which revelation is modified and distorted by its carriers in history, but they end by voiding it of any normative distinctiveness. At its final extension accommodationist attitudes to religion end in effective atheism, just as fundamentalists often end up in superstition. But Niebuhr points out that Liberal Christians are no more able to rid themselves of revelation than their opposite numbers can rid themselves of reason. Their thinking is ultimately logically dependent on the acceptance of a conviction that reason cannot give itself, which is the unique stature and significance of Jesus Christ.

And our two groups, radicals and liberals, fundamentalists and accommodationists, are again strangely alike in their attitude to evil and the tragic sense of life. Both groups incline to the side of law in dealing with the tension between theologies of Law and theologies of Grace. Since accommodationists are likely to be weak in their convictions about the possibility of the power of divine Grace for the healing and transforming of wounded lives, their tendency is to help the imperfect adjust to their imperfections, feel comfortable about themselves, rather than to encourage them to rely on the grace that can fulfil nature. Fundamentalists insist on the possibility of achievable human goodness: with enough effort we can learn to be good. Accommodationists tend to insist that we are good enough already, and with enough therapy we can learn to feel good. Neither group has any real need for the sublime and insane generosity of God's grace, God's free gift of his love as made known in Christ.

Almost certainly anyone who has tried to follow the way of Christ in all its challenge and paradox will be found somewhere on the continuum that stretches from fundamentalism to accommodationism. Its effect is to show the impact of Christ in the sweep of history. His troubling presence sets up a dynamic force in time that is self-correcting and self-critical. One resolution to the problem posed by his challenge to us leads inevitably to a restatement and later correction. Each generation gets it right and gets it wrong, so there is a provisional element in all Christian moral struggle that calls for a certain level of procedural humility from each of us. Christ has set up in history a great dialogue or controversy. He calls us to holiness and transcendence; he invites us to leap over the limitations of our time-bound and conditioned nature towards the perfection of God. Yet he recognizes our rootedness in time and society, our tethered-ness and limitedness, our need for constant acceptance and absolution. But he not only forgives our limitedness, he uses the very conditions that create it as a means of encounter with us. He calls to us from within history as well as from beyond it; he invites us to listen to it, to learn from it, as well as warning us not to be enslaved by it. Christ the Mystery of God encounters us through history and its particularity and limitedness, but his use of a particular epoch for that original and normative encounter operates according to the principles that tantalize us in all revelation: the divine encounter is mediated through the events and their particularity, but it is not to be limited by or identified with them, because that is to make the events themselves divine; it is to confer on the incidental accompaniments of the revealing encounter a trans-historical authority that is idolatrous. It is God in Christ we encounter through Jesus in that brief episode in Galilean history, but that obviously cannot make the cosmology, economic structures or political and social ideas of that era normative for all time. God always transcends time even as he uses it as a means of encounter with us, but the slip and slide of this encounter with God in time taxes our spiritual energies and disposes us to one of the false resolutions of the tension we have thought about in this chapter. We can trap ourselves in the illusionary certainties of the past and beach ourselves above the tides of history. Or we can cut ourselves off from the divine challenge that comes to us through the mediation of history and isolate ourselves in the present moment. Each approach is ultimately contemptuous of history and therefore deaf to God, for as T. S. Eliot reminded us:

> A people without history
> Is not redeemed from time, for history is a pattern
> Of timeless moments.[12]

It may be that the role of any single individual in this permanent controversy is unimportant, that what matters is the great argument itself, with all its distortions and corrections. Certainly, the reading of history remains a cordial for anyone who is depressed by the absurdities of any particular epoch. It does appear to be the case that the right balance is rarely found in individuals, though it does seem to emerge across generations. Nevertheless, certain types do seem to emerge, and at the extreme boundaries they define the debate. In theological terms we have thought of them as fundamentalists or accommodationists, but they exist in other areas as well and serve to define human debate in all its ramifications. Macauley, in describing the first appearance of the great political parties in England during the Long Parliament, captured the phenomenon in this way:

> From that day dates the corporate existence of the two great parties which have ever since alternately governed the country. In one sense, indeed, the distinction which then became obvious had always existed, and always must exist. For it has its origin in diversities of temper, of understanding, and of interest, which are found in all societies, and which will be found till the human mind ceases to be drawn in opposite directions by the charm of habit and by the charm of novelty. Not only in politics, but in literature, in art, in science, in surgery and mechanics, in navigation and agriculture, nay, even in mathematics, we find this distinction. Everywhere there is a class of men who cling with fondness to whatever is ancient, and who, even when convinced by overpowering reasons that innovation would be beneficial, consent to it with many misgivings and forebodings. We find also everywhere another class of men

sanguine in hope, bold in speculation, always pressing forward, quick to discern the imperfections of whatever exists, disposed to think lightly of the risks and inconveniences which attend improvements, and disposed to give every change credit for being an improvement. In the sentiments of both classes there is something to approve. But of both the best specimens will be found not far from the common frontier. The extreme section of one class consists of bigoted dotards: the extreme section of the other consists of shallow and reckless empirics.[13]

We probably need our bigoted dotards and our shallow and reckless empirics to outline the field of debate for us, but those who try to lead the examined life, the life that is open to all the paradoxes of a Divine Mystery that encounters us through our own history, will learn to live with less certainty than either group. But Christ will have released them from the tyrannous need to be right all the time. He will have liberated them to be daring and experimental in exploring their own nature and human culture, because he has called them to transcend themselves; but he will also have given them the strength to be cautious and the patience to wait, because he comes to them out of their own and humanity's past.

Living in the crossfire between the compulsion of opposing certainties will always be demanding, but it will not infrequently be exhilarating. Those who live out there sometimes get a sense from a long way off that they are hearing approving laughter. That is why they often stop and smile ruefully to themselves before crawling on. They may be far out in no-man's land, away from the big guns with their booming certainties, but they do learn to survive. And there's always that distant laughter. Faith has its conflicts, but it also has its mysterious consolations.

CODA
ON WORSHIP

What is left? The blissful responsibility to enjoy
the world.

Osip Mandelstam

I want to begin this postscript with some personal remin-
iscences. Several surveys on the subject, both in Britain and
America, reveal that a surprising number of men and women
have had what are best described as mystical experiences. The
term is loose and not very technical, but it does define an
experience of meaning and joy, a sense of seeing through to
the heart of reality, of capturing the sense of things in a flash
(though the experience may be much longer than that). I've
had several of these experiences and I would like to describe
two of them, though I do not make any great claims for
them: they are about as low on the Richter scale of mystical
experiences as it is possible to get.

The first happened when I was a curate in Glasgow about
thirty years ago. There was a theatre in the Gorbals, the
famous Citizens' Theatre, and they used to put on a pantomime every year's end. On the occasion to which I refer
the last scene in the pantomime was meant to be a sort of
representational, impressionistic tableau of life in Glasgow,
a typical day in fact, from dawn to dusk: it began with
workers going off to the shipyards (they still had them in
those days), moving down the dark streets, drawing on the
first cigarette of the day; then came the cleaning women with
their mops and pails, making for the big offices in the city;
then it was the milk- and paper-boys; then the school children,
some in the uniforms of private schools, most in the "grab-
anything" style of the ragged schools, trudging slowly to
school; then came the attractive young typists, drenched
in the scent of Drene Shampoo,[1] followed by men with
briefcases and bowler hats, the *Glasgow Herald* tucked under
their arms, with the stocks and shares columns already per-
used; and on it went, till I had my moment of vision. I caught
the sense of the whole city, the whole of life, as a great ballet

with everything in its place, everything intended, everything part of the meaning and rhythm of the whole created universe. I wanted to stand up and embrace everyone and tell them about the unity of it all, tell them about their own part in it, the steps only they could take. I wanted them to know that it all meant something, and something beautiful, so they must not be afraid and defensive; they must rejoice. That was my first low-grade mystical experience, though it can probably be dismissed as a Drene-induced hallucination.

The second was not unlike the first. I was hurrying down Shaftesbury Avenue in London one afternoon about fifteen years later, when everything went into slow-motion. Before I went over this particular threshold everything was rushed and untidy and without a pattern, a meaningless jostle of people and buses and traffic policemen, a sordid urban jungle; but over the threshold, into the experience, the moment the slow-motion switch was thrown, everything changed, and again it was a ballet I perceived, a pattern I descried, meaning I discovered. The traffic policeman was conducting a great dance and every part was spontaneous, yet pre-arranged; nothing was without meaning, yet everything was free. And again I wanted to embrace it all and have it all embraced because we were all a great company, a dance company, a family ballet, not a crowd of strangers, and why could not everyone see that? I saw it in that flash, and continued my way down the street grinning affectionately at everyone I met, oblivious to the strange looks and wide berths I received.

I have often wondered about those experiences and one or two others, in the words of the Orcadian poet, Edwin Muir:

Was it a delusion?
Or did we see that day the unseeable
Sole glory of the everlasting world
Perpetually at work, though never seen
Since Eden locked the gate that's everywhere
And nowhere?[2]

When I am brave enough and faithful enough I know they were not delusions, not abnormal, but the right way to see, the truly normal vision, the thing I would see always if my eyes were not holden, like those of the two who walked to Emmaus and failed to recognize the one who walked with them. There seem to be two ways of looking at the world, two valid but different ways of seeing, but most of us have lost one of them. There is, first of all and most obviously, what is called "objective consciousness". This is a way of seeing that is detached and uninvolved: I am in here, in myself, inside my head, and the world lies out there as an object and I examine it. Objective consciousness is detached, clinical, neutral. The other way of seeing I shall call "contemplation" and it is quite unlike objective consciousness: it is passionate, attached, at one with what it beholds, seeing with the subjectivity and involvement of the lover watching the beloved caught in an unself-conscious moment; or with that heart-stopping tenderness every parent knows when the beloved child, for instance, is up in front of an audience of strangers to sing or recite, or when you catch sight of him, unaware of you, as he is victimized or picked on by the school bullies. In contemplation you are at one with what you behold, and everything is enlarged and widened and loaded with significance.

We need each way of seeing. Without objective consciousness there would be no science, because it is the task of objective consciousness to perceive connections, see how things work, observe dispassionately the laws of operation, watch all the bits interacting and enmeshing. Objective consciousness sees the trees, but contemplation sees the whole wood and is at one with it; it sees the beauty, the ballet, the dance of the trees, the totality of the wood and is in some passionate way at one with it, or would like to be, longs to be, if only it could unself itself. Objective consciousness breaks things down to see how they work, while contemplation unites things, creates unities, puts things together, gathers up the fragments, losing nothing.

Both ways of seeing have their place, but it is holistic vision, contemplation, the perception of the unities, that is at risk in our society and that we need to rediscover and re-affirm if we are to be whole people. And worship and prayer are about that way of seeing: they are about play not work, wholeness not dismemberment; they are about the singleness and intensity of Eternity, not about the successiveness and boredom of time; they are about Madness and Mystery, not carefulness and control (the paradox being, of course, that they frequently become arenas for the playing out of power games and the exerting of control). Blake caught the difference perfectly in these ways of seeing in his famous exclamation:

"What," it will be questioned, "when the sun rises, do you not see a round disc of fire somewhat like a guinea?" "O no, no, I see an innumerable company of the heavenly host crying, 'Holy, Holy, Holy is the Lord God Almighty'."[3]

But this important distinction and the experiences that lie behind it are not confined to the strictly religious sphere. We are up against a contrast, an experience that runs right through life. The best way I can think of to explore this contrast and its significance is to examine the ancient philosophical distinction in the meaning of the word "good". There are two kinds of good in human experience; what philosophers call "instrumental good" and "intrinsic good". In other words, some things are good *for* something else and some things are simply *good* in themselves. "Guinness is good *for* you", the old advertisement used to say: Guinness is not good in itself, it is good *for* you, it builds you up if you are devitamined, it gives you a pleasant sensation of well-being if you drink enough of it; it is an instrumental good, good for something other than itself. But there are other kinds of good that are intrinsically good just for their own sake, and they derive their nature from the Highest Good: God is simply good in himself; not an instrument, a lever, a means to some other end, but an end, the end, the Good in and for and through himself. As I say, some things derive their nature from that Good, have something of its flavour. Music, for instance, is an intrinsic good; we play it, not because it is good for musicians and their bank accounts, or good for the makers of musical instruments, or the producers of records and hi-fi equipment, but because music is in and for itself something that is simply good, done for its own sake. Intrinsic goods are things we celebrate, while instrumental goods are things we manipulate. Instrumental goods are all means to some other end, while intrinsic goods are enjoyed for their own sake. Prayer in its essence is an intrinsic good: it is not done for any reason other than itself. It is not, at its essential heart, a means to any other end: it is not done to wrest concessions from God – health, possessions, spiritual well-being; it is simply the attention drawn from us by the beauty of God; it is our inclination towards God; it has no purpose other than that of simple regard, simple attention upon the one who draws us. Prayer is useless otherwise, has no real human function, does not get us anything; indeed, it rejoices in this complete absence of motive:

> My God, I love thee; not because
>   I hope for heaven thereby,
> Nor yet because who love thee not
>   Are lost eternally.
>
> Not with the hope of gaining aught,
>   Not seeking a reward;
> But as thyself hast loved me,
>   O ever-loving Lord!
>
> E'en so I love thee, and will love,
>   And in thy praise will sing,
> Solely because thou art my God,
>   And my eternal king.[4]

So there are two ways of seeing the world and two ways of acting within the world, and the ways of seeing are related to the ways of acting. One way of operating gives us control or power; it is always done for the sake of something else. It is the fixed eye of someone figuring the angles, seeking to understand and manipulate the situation. Or it is the eye of the lover simply gazing, the action of the celebrant simply doing the thing for its own sake. And the fascination in all this is that one can shade into the other; things that we do for a reason, instrumental goods, by virtue of some impulse in us, end by being done for the sake of being done; they become prized for their own sake, become goods in themselves. We no longer buy stamps simply to stick on letters, but because they have become strangely desirable in their own right. We no longer clothe ourselves simply to cover our nakedness; the clothes themselves become something we like, something we wear for their own sake: the soberly dressed civil servant is not going to use the gaily spotted handkerchief that is tucked into his lapel pocket – it is there for its own sake, makes its own statement, is a little flourish in its own right.

In other words, human beings have a mysterious, built-in genius for turning means into ends, for taking some entirely practical activity (an instrumental good), which is done for the sake of something else, and turning it into something that is done for its own sake. It is as though we had an instinct for imposing value on things in themselves, giving worth to them, transmuting the use of them from something functional, something that is only a way of getting something else, into something that is itself of immense significance. That whole dynamic is called *Worship*, the giving of worth to something, the celebration of its value, its uniqueness, its absolute adorability. Worship with a small "W" is something that is done for the fun of it, the sheer nonsense and spectacle.

Trooping the Colour is a good example. Originally a regimental standard, or colour, was paraded round the soldiers just before a battle. Trooping the Colour was a serious and practical matter that served to help soldiers recognize it when the need arose in the confusion and dust of battle. Those days have long passed but we still do it. The difference is that nowadays we do it because we enjoy doing it. It has become something we do for its own sake. It adds a tone and texture to life, which would be very dull without these superfluous flourishes, these little acts of pure worship. In a sense, the British monarchy is another example, although here there are quite a few practical advantages as well. One of the main uses of the monarchy is to supply a means of expressing our need for colour and pageantry, and to provide a focus for our self-awareness as a nation. Of course, there are always many people who are against all these things. They are usually people of a dour and puritan disposition, natural commissars, who think that life ought to be stripped of all these unnecessary flourishes and reduced to strict geometric logic, the result of unremitting Objective Consciousness. We often find them in churches, people who would like our worship stripped of all its delicious inessentials and reduced to dull earnestness, not knowing that the worship instinct itself is the source of all this frivolity. It is the *unnecessary* things we *need* if we are to be fully human: we need poetry and music and custom and ceremony and all the sheer wonderful nonsense of simply being alive. We must be protected from all the commissars in our midst who would deprive us of our baubles. W. B. Yeats captures what I'm trying to say in the last stanza of his poem, *A Prayer for My Daughter*:

> and may her bridegroom bring her to a house
> Where all's accustomed, ceremonious;
> For arrogance and hatred are the wares
> Peddled in the thoroughfares.
> How but in custom and in ceremony
> Are innocence and beauty born?
> Ceremony's a name for the rich horn,
> And custom for the spreading laurel tree.[5]

Now Christian worship, especially within the Catholic tradition, takes this impulse, this instinct towards the elaboration of means into ends, and develops and expresses it sometimes to an unbearably beautiful degree. Modern liturgies, because of their very newness, have lost something of this intricate and lovely complexity. The more ancient tendency was towards a kind of richness that sought to express and respond to the sheer extravagance and prodigality of God, the kind of divine theatricality that the contemplative eye sees in those moments of vision, captured by Robinson Jeffers:

> Is it not by his high superfluousness we know
> Our God? For to equal a need
> Is natural, animal, mineral: but to fling
> Rainbows over the rain
> And beauty above the moon, and secret rainbows
> On the domes of deep sea-shells,
> And make necessary embrace of breeding
> Beautiful also as fire,

Not even the weeds to multiply without blossom
Nor the birds without music . . .[6]

So Worship celebrates the beauty of God, the sheer *Is*ness of
his being, the absolute centrality of his simply being there and
being adorable. We are not figuring the angle or estimating the
height and putting the hard question (there is another time
and place for that); we are looking and exclaiming, watching
the ballet, caught out of ourselves by the opera, unself-
consciously taking our part in the dance. That is the big
impulse, the central dynamic, the main theme; but that theme,
that push towards the absolute, that impulse that forces us to
take things we do for a reason and do them for their own
sake, begins to take over, so the big theme gets repeated in a
variety of little sub-themes. We have to walk from here to
there and that is how we begin; then we give it a bit of a
glide; then we elaborate the glide a turn or two, and soon we
have made the walk a dance. Words have to be said, so we
say them and like the sound and say them again, and give
them a lilt and a modulation and before we know it we are
singing, and multiplying sound upon sound, singing upon
singing, creating harmonies, piling it on, making the necessary the mother of gloriously unnecessary profusion. It is
useful now to have someone on an instrument to help us keep
the notes, so we start with a whistle and end with a five
manual organ or a whole orchestra. And think of the vast and
wasteful torrents of music that have been poured out down
the ages. Alan Watts says this of Bach, for instance:

> The preludes and fugues . . . are simply a complex arrange-
> ment of glorious sounds . . . They need no programme
> notes to explain a moral or sociological message . . . The
> intricate melodies flow on and on, and there never seems
> any necessity for them to stop. He composed them in
> tremendous quantities, with the same Godlike extravagance
> to be found in the unnecessary vastness of nature.

And we find the same elaborating impulse at work in the use
of space. We start in the front room and we add a candle and
a posy of flowers; then we hire the baker's loft and someone

paints it up and carves a few things on the beams, and soon we decide to build something just for the liturgy; our imagination is really caught and we have moved from the front parlour to Chartres by the same dynamic. At first we get into our Sunday best, priest and deacons, readers and prophets, and one day young Father Isaac throws a brightly coloured scarf over his toga and blushes but sticks to his instincts, and we end up with the richness and variety of liturgical vesture in all its pointless but captivating exuberance.

That is the dynamic; it is what we might call the logic of adoration, the sheer almost ungovernable impulse to give worth and value to something; but it is grounded in God and the magnetic effect of his beauty, drawing us into understanding, out of ourselves into vision of the meaning of all things; prompting us to catch the sweep and scale of the dance of creation. When we come to Christian Worship, therefore, it is not Objective Consciousness we must bring, that impulse to analyse and question and criticize and notice everything except the important thing. What is needed is the kind of consciousness we call prayer and contemplation:

> You are not here to verify,
> Instruct yourself, or inform curiosity
> Or carry report. You are here to kneel
> Where prayer has been valid. And prayer is more
> Than an order of words, the conscious occupation
> Of the praying mind, or the sound of the voice praying.[7]

An American priest once described worship at the Church of the Advent in Boston as "Grand Opera or a Kiss" and that, it seems to me, is what Christian liturgy is about. It can range from the theatricality of grand opera, with all the sweep and range and extravagance (and not a little of the unconscious humour that often characterizes the more earnest passages) of some grand production, right over to the quietness and intimacy of a lover's embrace. A particular service can be anywhere on that line but, and this is the most intriguing part of the thing, both elements can be found in the grandest services: intimacy and grandeur, epic sweep and quiet ordinariness.

We find both these elements in our relationship with God. God is sublime, overwhelming and inaccessible like a great range of mountains dwarfing a tiny climber seen from miles away in the clear light, slowly trudging up a pass. There is that in God which calls forth awe, and the visionary moment gives us a glimpse into that grandness, that vast hinterland of pure being and sheer love and power, kept in the repose of gentleness; and sometimes our worship captures just the fringe of that reality. It is why we keep our grand buildings and our great organs and those treble voices that break our hearts as they rise and hit the great vaulted roofs. They are a feeble but instinctive attempt to respond to the divine sublimity. Yet that vast and depthless God is closer to us than our own breathing; *is* our own breathing. God is the quiet at the moment after the words of consecration, the space between the notes, the hush that follows the last note of the most glorious postlude played by the best musician on the grandest organ in the universe – grand opera or a kiss. In praying the liturgy we have to attend to both: spectacle and intimacy; beauty contrived and ordered, as well as the freedom and play of lovers. Worship tantalizes us and frustrates our prayer because we can never hold it for long, never possess it. It eludes us and escapes just at the moment before clarity, and that is why we keep coming back. Dostoevsky said, "*Beauty will redeem the world*", but the beauty is never owned by us, never pinned down, so the redemption is not yet complete, only promised, hinted at, sometimes almost delivered; but then the clock starts again, the dance falls back into ordinary chaos, the moment of vision passes and all we see is traffic. Did we ever see anything else? That is the question we must live with.

That is the question we must live with, but there are one or two spiritual strategies that will help us in the living. In praying the liturgy (which is the name we give to the structures of Christian Worship that have evolved over the centuries under the elaborating impulses I have described), it is adoration, the pouring out of ourselves in amazement and longing towards the great beauty that haunts us either as

reality or as loss, that is the core of the thing; and Mary of
Bethany is the great scriptural exemplar, pouring and oozing
that pound of precious ointment upon the feet of Jesus.

> Six days before the Passover, Jesus came to Bethany, where
> Lazarus was, whom Jesus had raised from the dead. There
> they made him a supper; Martha served, and Lazarus was
> one of those at table with him. Mary took a pound of costly
> ointment of pure nard and anointed the feet of Jesus and
> wiped his feet with her hair; and the house was filled with
> the fragrance of the ointment. But Judas Iscariot, one of his
> disciples (he who was to betray him), said "Why was this
> ointment not sold for three hundred denarii and given to
> the poor?" This he said, not that he cared for the poor but
> because he was a thief, and as he had the money box he
> used to take what was put into it. Jesus said, "Let her alone,
> let her keep it for the day of my burial. The poor you
> always have with you, but you do not always have me."[8]

"Prodigal waste," said Judas, "all that money gone!" Exactly!
Something beautiful for God, the ancient impulse to give
away, to stop calculating and measuring and simply to surrender. But is not adoration something that simply happens,
something that surprises us, something beyond our own
contriving? Yes, and that is why we must try to *pray* the
liturgy. Fortunately, the liturgy goes on without us, the dance
continues even if we are distracted; it has an objectivity that
operates apart from our perception of it: all the works of the
Lord praise the Lord whether or not we acknowledge it. But
it is by praying that we join in, try to lift up our own hearts
onto the great stream of worship that is ascending all around
us. Prayer is simply the name we give to our own efforts to
join in what is happening, to bring our minds to attention, to
try to concentrate.

And we must not be afraid of the distractions that crowd
into our minds, the long stretches when we do not concentrate
at all, when we come-to suddenly, realizing that the communion of the people has started already and our minds were
miles away. We must pull ourselves back gently and must
not belabour ourselves with guilt, because we are certain that

we are the only ones there with wandering thoughts – or worse. There is that Mrs Gush who always looks so serene and holy and utterly concentrated – well, she spent the whole of the liturgy figuring out how to redecorate the back bedroom now that her daughter Sue is married. And Father Smallhip, who looks positively beatific up there in the sanctuary, is fighting hard against carnal imaginings that feature Marlene Sweetbreath, the new contralto in the choir. We are all fighting hard for even a minute's concentration, and that fight is prayer, including the breast-beating and remorse.

Bishop Michael Ramsey was asked how much time he spent each day at his private devotions and he replied: "Half an hour. I only pray for a minute, but it takes me twenty-nine minutes to get there." As with any type of prayer, technique is important, and technique is simply a way of recognizing our need for structure and support in trying to concentrate. It helps if the celebrant builds moments of silence into the liturgy when we can bring our minds back to attention. I particularly value silence before the confession for a minute; a bit of time at the Offertory to get my mind together; and a minute at the end of the consecration prayer: little checkpoints, as it were, when we can bring our minds back to the business in hand. Sometimes our prayer may only be those three minutes and the rest a jumble of distraction, but that *is* prayer, and we are not to fret over it. Properly ordered worship will help us to pray the liturgy, but it is possible to pray the liturgy in spite of the insensitivity of some clergy who make no concessions to the human needs of their congregations. When I was a horrid young high church prig we used to rate a priest's soundness by the speed with which he celebrated the liturgy, because we were anxious to stress its objectivity. But that is as big a distortion as its opposite, when we get self-indulgent worship on the part of the celebrant, full of false theatricality and devotionalism. Since the Liturgy is *common* prayer it must have something of the highest *common* factor about it, something that makes it accessible to the maximum number of people. That means it will have to steer something of a middle way between excessive subjectivity and excessive objectivity, between viewing the liturgy, on the one hand, as a sort of sacramental dispensing machine, a eucharistomat, and, on the other hand, as a sort of sentimental orgy in which we chase one another all over the nave with giggles and grunts and shouts of glee. Balance is the secret, balance enough to keep both the over-emotional and the under-emotional in an equilibrium of mutual dissatisfaction.

★

Let me, in conclusion, turn briefly to something I have not discussed. We might be forgiven for feeling that so far I have offered a sort of rosy, ageing-hippy, go-with-the-flow-Joe theology of liturgy, in which the universe is really a great barn-dance of joy and all we have to do is switch on to it. Well, that is part of what I am trying to say. There is a dance, but all dancers cast a shadow and there is a great shadow over God's universe. Theologians call this realization the Fall and they mean by that that the universe is bent, flawed, biased; that good is in constant contention with evil and that it is not an easy conflict. There is a power of evil in the universe that penetrates even to the sanctuary of God: in a small way we feel that struggle by our fitful attentions to God, our inability to concentrate on the liturgy for more than seconds; but we feel it more profoundly as we contemplate realistically our own flaws and failures, the evil we have done and the good we have left undone; the lack of energy for holiness in our lives, the inevitable settling for comfort and moderation, rather than reaching for the heroic and the strong. We know all that about ourselves, and we see it multiplied into terrible conflicts between the millions of competing egotisms that compose human history, from the snigger behind the lace curtains at that silly woman next door, down to the industrial-ized sadism of the Holocaust or the impenetrable hatreds in Ulster. That is all in the Liturgy, too, and must not be banished. The confession of sins must not be a reflex sort of action: "So sorry I'm late, darling", as we hang up our coats. It must be honest and searching, genuine confession.

And our intercessions must not be trite little travelogues of international trouble spots: something of the horror and anguish of God must be in them, something hard and objec-tive, and there was maybe more of that in the old intercessions than in some of the new. But the real focus of the Fall in the liturgy is at the same place as the focus on God's great redeeming mercy and pity: it is at the consecration prayer as we celebrate, re-present, the death and passion of Jesus. That is the silence that lies at the heart of it all; it is something we see from an immense distance but with amazing clarity. We see a dying, an eternal dying, away off there at the very heart of things, from the foundation of the world. It has the silence of something we see from a great distance, the clarity of something at hand. And it is an event that baffles and compels us, a vortex that draws away the sins of the world. That is why Christians continue to make eucharist, to give thanks in the midst of tragedy, because it has all been taken care of by the lamb standing there, slain from the foundation of the earth. Eucharistic Joy! Not, perhaps, the most conspicuous characteristic of contemporary Christianity – but it ought to be.

The best things can never be said too often, so let me end by quoting some words I quote at every available opportunity. They were written by a Russian poet, hounded to death by Stalin in 1938:

> *Christian art is joyous because it is free, and it is free because of the fact of Christ's having died to redeem the world. One need not die in art nor save the world in it, those matters having been, so to speak, attended to. What is left? The blissful responsibility to enjoy the world.*[9]

NOTES

Part One: THE WHITE GARDEN

I The White Garden

1 Nigel Nicolson, *Portrait of a Marriage*, Bantam Books, 1974, p. 242.
2 Evelyn Underhill, *Letters*, Longmans, Green, 1956, p. 165.

II The Accusation

1 T. S. Eliot, *Notes towards the Definition of Culture*, Faber & Faber, p. 19.
2 Patrick Reilly, *George Orwell: The Age's Adversary*, Macmillan, 1986, p. 61.
3 Judges 17:6

III The Window

1 Robert Browning, *A Grammarian's Funeral*.
2 Northrop Frye, *The Great Code*, Harcourt Brace, New York & London, 1982, pp. 41, 42.
3 Wesley Ariarajah, *The Bible and People of Other Faiths*, W.C.C., 1985, pp. 25–7.
4 Sermo 5, 6–8 in *Patrologia Latina, 36*, cols. 57–59 cited in G. Martelet *The Risen Christ and the Eucharistic Word*, Collins, 1976.
5 William Shakespeare, *The Merchant of Venice*, III, i, 63.
6 David Edwards, *The Futures of Christianity*, Hodder and Stoughton, 1987, pp. 276–7.

IV The Word

1 Walter Wink, *Transforming Bible Study*, Abingdon, 1980, p. 155.
2 Walter Wink, *ibid.*

Part Two: ENCOUNTERING THE MYSTERY

V Gethsemane

1 Psalm 130:1.
2 Psalm 69:1
3 Lamentations 1:1–2
4 Lamentations 1:12
5 Jeremiah 31:15
6 Richard Holloway, *The Way of the Cross*, Fount, 1987, p. 71.
7 Mark 14:32–42.
8 T. S. Eliot, *Burnt Norton*.

9   Mark 10:17–22.
10 *Confessions* VIII.

VI Jerusalem

1   William Shakespeare,
    Othello, II, i.
2   Peter Gomes. From a
    sermon preached at
    Harvard University on
    9th December 1984.
3   Genesis 3:1–14, 23.
4   Luke 22:31–34, 54–62.
5   Revelation 12:7–9.
6   Milton, *Paradise Lost*.
    Book 1, 247.
7   Matthew 27:1, 11–14, 24,
    26.
8   Numbers 25:1–13
9   Paul Johnson, *A History of
    the Jews*, Weidenfeld and
    Nicolson, 1987, p. 122.
10 Luke 23:34.

VII Golgotha

1   Luke 23:33–49.

VIII Galilee

1   Pascal, *Pensées*.
2   W. H. Auden, *Modern
    Canterbury Pilgrims*, 1956,
    p. 41.
3   Mark 5:4–5.
4   Colossians 1:15, 19
5   John 21:4–9, 12, 15–22.
6   Mark 8:27–36.
7   Mark 9:2–8.
8   John 18:3–11.
9   John 3:16–17.
10 Luke 7:36–47.
11 Galatians 2:11–14.

12 Acts of the Apostles 5:1–11.
13 Albert Schweitzer, *The
    Quest of the Historical Jesus*,
    Third Edition, 1954,
    p. 400. SCM Press,
    reissued 1981.
14 Albert Schweitzer, *ibid*,
    p. 401.

IX Crossfire

1   Adrian Hastings, *A History
    of English Christianity,
    1920–85*, Collins, 1986.
2   Edwin Muir, "One Foot in
    Eden", from *The Collected
    Poems*, Faber & Faber.
3   Schweitzer, *ibid*.
4   Schweitzer, *ibid*.
5   Richard Niebuhr, *Christ and
    Culture*, Harper, New
    York, 1956, especially
    Chapters 1–3.
6   Niebuhr, op. cit., pp. 39–40.
7   Schweitzer, *ibid*.
8   Rebecca West, *The Birds
    Fall Down*, London,
    Macmillan, 1966.
9   Niebuhr, op. cit., p. 66.
10 Niebuhr, *ibid*.
11 Niebuhr, op. cit., p. 67.
12 T. S. Eliot, *Little Gidding*.
13 Macaulay, *The History of
    England*, Vol. 1., pp. 96, 97.

CODA ON WORSHIP

1   Or so I seem to remember.
    John Betjeman sang of
    Elaine who: "Hiding hair
    which, Friday nightly

delicately drowns in Drene".

2 Edwin Muir, "Transfigur-ation" from *The Collected Poems of Edwin Muir*, Faber & Faber.

3 Blake, *Descriptive Catalogue*, 1810. The Vision of Judgement.

4 *English Hymnal* No. 80.

5 W. B. Yeats, "A Prayer for My Daughter", from *The Collected Poems of W. B. Yeats*.

6 Robinson Jeffers, *Be Angry at the Sun*, Random House, New York, 1941.

7 T. S. Eliot, *ibid*.

8 John 12:1–8.

9 Nadezhda Mandelstam, *Hope Against Hope*, London, Collins and Harvill Press, 1971, p. X.